Talawa Theatre Company, Soho ...ie Albany
present

GOD'S PROPERTY

by Arinze Kene

The first preview of God's Property was at the Albany, Deptford, on 20th February 2013

God's Property had its world premiere on 26th February 2013 at Soho Theatre

Talawa Theatre Company, Soho Theatre and the Albany are supported by Arts Council England

Supported using public funding by
ARTS COUNCIL
LOTTERY FUNDED **ENGLAND**

CAST

Kingsley Ben-Adir
Bradley Gardner
Ash Hunter
Ria Zmitrowicz

CREATIVE AND PRODUCTION TEAM

Arinze Kene	Writer
Michael Buffong	Director
Ellen Cairns	Designer
Jason Taylor	Lighting Designer
Jack C Arnold	Sound Designer
Dennis Charles	Production Manager
Vanessa Sutherland	Company Stage Manager
Naomi Hill	Deputy Stage Manager

CAST

KINGSLEY BEN-ADIR CHIMA
Kingsley graduated from the Guildhall School of Music and Drama in 2011. Theatre credits include: *A Midsummer Night's Dream* directed by Matthew Dunster (Regent's Park Open Air Theatre); *The Riots* directed by Nicolas Kent (Tricycle Theatre and Bernie Grant Arts Centre); *The Westbridge* directed by Clint Dyer (Royal Court Theatre); *Two Gentlemen of Verona* directed by Matthew Dunster (Royal & Derngate); *Blue/Orange* directed by Karen Henson (Middlesborough Theatre). Television credits include: *Marple: A Caribbean Mystery* (ITV). Film credits include: *The Rat's Routine, City Slacker* and *World War Z* (Paramount Pictures/Plan B Entertainment). He was a finalist for the Michael Bryant Award in 2011.

BRADLEY GARDNER LIAM
Bradley was born in the North East and brought up in the New Forest before moving to London to train at Italia Conti. Theatre credits include: *Year 10* (Finborough/BAC/French theatre festival tour; *Time Out* critics' choice); *Big Love* directed by Mallissa Kievman and Thea Sharrock (Gate Theatre, Notting Hill); *East and West United* (Soho Theatre); *Saved* (Lyric, Hammersmith). Television and film credits include: *Criminal Justice, Half Broken Things, Doctors, Casualty* (BBC); *The Bill*; Neil Maskel's *Shitkicker*; *Q's Fever* (Sony films); *Rites of Passage* (Lime Pictures).

ASH HUNTER ONOCHIE

Ash Hunter graduated from Central School of Speech and Drama in 2011. Theatre credits include: *A Midsummer Night's Dream* (Almeida Theatre); *Gravity* (Birmingham Rep); *A Clockwork Orange* directed by Dawn Reid (Theatre Royal Stratford East). Television and radio credits include: *Switch* (ITV2); *One Million Tiny Plays* (BBC Radio 4).

RIA ZMITROWICZ HOLLY

Ria trained with the National Youth Theatre. Theatre credits include: *Chapel Street,* which won the Emerging Talent Award in Edinburgh in 2012, before transferring to the Bush Theatre; *Skanky* (Arcola Theatre); *The Grandfathers* (Ovalhouse Theatre); *The Site* (Roundhouse); *Routes* (Hampstead Theatre). Television credits include: *Whitechapel*; *Youngers* (E4). She will soon been seen in *Murder on the Homefront* (ITV1).

CREATIVE AND PRODUCTION TEAM

ARINZE KENE WRITER

Arinze Kene was named most promising playwright by Off West End.com (Offies) for his debut play *Estate Walls* which ran at the Ovalhouse Theatre, London. English Touring Theatre's co-production of his play *Little Baby Jesus* was nominated for two Off West End Theatre Awards – Best New Play and Best Male Performer. He was also shortlisted for the Alfred Fagon Award in 2009. Arinze was a member of the Young Writers' Programme at the Royal Court Theatre and part of the 2012 Supergroup, during which time he wrote *Hoop and Harm*. He has been a member of Soho Theatre's Young Writers Group and participated in their HUB writers' programme. He was one of the inaugural Soho Six, a selected group of six writers who are commissioned and are in residency for a six-month period to work on a new play for Soho Theatre. During his residency Arinze wrote *God's Property*. Kene is part of the writing team on E20 for *EastEnders*/BBC. In 2012, he was a Pearson Writer-in-Residence at Lyric Theatre, Hammersmith. Arinze's play *Hackney Baths* was broadcast on BBC Radio 4 during the London Olympics. He has just completed writing a film for Film London entitled *Seekers*.

MICHAEL BUFFONG DIRECTOR

Michael is the Artistic Director of Talawa Theatre Company, Britain's primary Black-led theatre company. Theatre credits include: *The Serpent's Tooth* (Talawa Theatre Company and Almeida Theatre); *Moon on a Rainbow Shawl* (National Theatre); the multi-award winning *A Raisin in the Sun*, *Private Lives*, *All the Ordinary Angels*, *Six Degrees of Separation*, *On My*

Birthday (Royal Exchange, Manchester); *One Flew Over the Cuckoo's Nest* (Curve, Leicester); *Crawling in the Dark* (Almeida Theatre); *To Kill a Mockingbird* (West Yorkshire Playhouse/Birmingham Rep); *Little Sweet Thing* (Hampstead Theatre); *Raising the Roof* (Palace Theatre Shaftesbury Avenue); *Long Time No See, Unfinished Business* (Talawa Theatre Company); *Souls* (Theatre Centre); *The Prayer* (Young Vic Studio); *Stories from Mean Street* (New End Theatre, Hampstead); *Airport 2000* (Leicester Haymarket); *Brother to Brother* (Lyric Hammersmith); *Scrape of the Black* (Theatre Royal Stratford East); *In Pieces* (Coventry Belgrade). Television and film credits include: *Holby City, EastEnders, Admin, Placebo, Calais Rules, Doctors, Casualty, Comedy Shuffle* (BBC); *Hollyoaks* (Lime Pictures); *Feeling It* (Eye2Eye); *Blazed* (Channel 4); *Simple!* (Acapulco Film Festival).

ELLEN CAIRNS DESIGNER

Ellen Cairns trained at Glasgow School of Art and The Slade and was a recipient of an Arts Council Theatre Design Bursary. She has been a freelance designer since 1989 and designs extensively in this country and abroad. Previous productions for Talawa include: *O, Babylon, The Dragon Can't Dance, The Importance of Being Earnest, Medea in the Mirror* and *King Lear*. Recent productions with Michael Buffong directing are *A Raisin in The Sun* and *Private Lives* at Royal Exchange, Manchester, and *One Flew Over the Cuckoo's Nest* at Curve, Leicester. Current productions include: an outdoor performance at Linlithgow Palace of *A Satire of the Three Estates*, productions of *Les Misérables* in Finland and Denmark, and costumes for *The Phantom of the Opera* in Estonia.

JASON TAYLOR LIGHTING DESIGNER

Jason has extensive experience lighting for theatre both in the UK and internationally. His previous work for Talawa includes: *The Colored Museum* and *Rum and Coca Cola*. His many West End credits include: *Our Boys* (West End); *Journey's End* (West End/Broadway; Tony Award-nominated for Best Lighting Design); *Top Girls* (West End/Chichester); *The Rivals* (West End/Bath); *Rainman, Absurd Person Singular, Duet for One, High Society, Rosencrantz and Guildenstern Are Dead* and *Abigail's Party*. In addition he has lit numerous productions for the National Theatre, Royal Court, Old Vic, Menier Chocolate Factory, Hampstead Theatre, and most of the leading regional theatres. He has lit twenty seasons at Regent's Park Open Air Theatre where productions include: *A Midsummer Night's Dream, Richard III, Romeo and Juliet, Kiss Me Kate, Troilus and Cressida, Hamlet* and *The Pirates of Penzance*. His many national tours include: *The Rise and Fall of Little Voice, Doctor in the House, Season's Greetings, Flashdance, Dancing at Lughnasa, The Surprise Party, Lady Be Good* and *The Hobbit*. International credits include: *Love Never Dies* (Copenhagen); *The Merry Wives of Windsor* (Globe Theatre USA/UK tour); *Pygmalion* (Broadway); *Sweet Sorrow* (Los Angeles); *Blood Brothers* (Australia/New Zealand).

JACK C ARNOLD COMPOSER AND SOUND DESIGNER

Jack is a film, theatre and television music composer and sound designer. Recent theatre credits include: *Buried Child, The Lieutenant of Inishmore* and *One Flew Over the Cuckoo's Nest* at Curve, Leicester. Other theatre credits include: Simon Bent's hit adaptation of *Elling*, Colin Teevan's *Missing Persons: Four Tragedies and Roy Keane* and Justin Butcher's *The Madness of George*

Dubya, all in the West End. Jack received an RTS nomination in 2012 for Best Score for the TV comedy drama *Holy Flying Circus*. He scored the supernatural series *Demons* for ITV1; the international Emmy Award-winning *The Beckoning Silence* for Channel 4, and contributed additional music to Shane Meadow's series *This is England '86* as well as many other programmes for BBC, ITV, Channel 4, Discovery and National Geographic. Jack has scored two feature films: *The Scouting Book for Boys* (Celador Films), directed by long-time collaborator Tom Harper, and *Albatross* (CinemaNX) directed by Niall MacCormick.

Talawa
Theatre Company

'Talawa has an impressive legacy – making theatre that people of any colour would queue round the block to see.' *Time Out*

Talawa Theatre Company is Britain's primary Black-led theatre company, founded in 1986 by Yvonne Brewster, Mona Hammond, Carmen Munroe and Inigo Espejel.

Since its inception Talawa has mounted African, Caribbean, American and British classics and exciting new writing, and performed the work of writers such as C.L.R. James, Derek Walcott, Michael Abbensetts, Wole Soyinka, George C. Wolfe, Michael Bhim, Arinze Kene and Mustapha Matura.

A number of Britain's finest actors, many of whom have gone on to successful careers in film, radio, theatre and television, have worked with Talawa including Norman Beaton, Cathy Tyson, Don Warrington, Nonso Anozie, Martina Laird, Danny John-Jules and Mona Hammond.

As well as producing work with high-profile established practitioners and delivering productions that have a major impact on the British theatrical landscape, Talawa also develops the talents of new Black actors, writers and directors.

The Company runs an extensive participation and education programme that includes TYPT, our integrated season for emerging theatre-makers, and a range of outreach activities that include bespoke workshops for all ages and abilities, which are curriculum-based, artistic or related to participants' personal and social development.

Michael Buffong was appointed as Talawa Theatre Company's Artistic Director in 2012.

For the latest information on our work go to www.talawa.com and keep in touch with the Company through Facebook (TalawaTheatreCompany) and Twitter (TalawaTheatreCo).

TALAWA STAFF
Artistic Director **Michael Buffong**
Executive Producer **Christopher Rodriguez**
Administrator **Havana Wellings Longmore**
Finance Officer **Zewditu Bekele**
Participation and Education Officer **Gail Babb**
Marketing and Press Manager **Jackie Friend**
Press Representative **James Lever at Target Live**

53–55 East Road
London N1 6AH
020 7251 6644

Talawa Theatre Company gratefully acknowledges the support of Arts Council England.
Registered Charity No: 327362

Supported using public funding by
ARTS COUNCIL
ENGLAND
LOTTERY FUNDED

London's most vibrant venue for new writing, comedy and cabaret.

Bang in the creative heart of London, Soho Theatre is a major new-writing theatre and a writers' development organisation of national significance. With a programme spanning theatre, comedy, cabaret and writers' events and home to a lively bar, Soho Theatre is one of the most vibrant venues on London's cultural scene.

Soho Theatre owns its own central London venue housing the intimate 150-seat Soho Theatre, our 90-seat Soho Upstairs and our new 1950s New York meets Berliner cabaret space, Soho Downstairs. Under the joint leadership of Soho's Artistic Director Steve Marmion and Executive Director Mark Godfrey, Soho Theatre now welcomes over 150,000 people a year.

'Soho Theatre was buzzing, and there were queues all over the building as audiences waited to go into one or other of the venue's spaces. I spend far too much time in half-empty theatres to be cross at the sight of an audience, particularly one that is so young, exuberant and clearly anticipating a good time.' Lyn Gardner, *Guardian*

SOHO THEATRE BAR
Soho Theatre Bar is a buzzy, fun bar where artists and performers can regularly be seen pint in hand enjoying the company of friends and fans. Open from 9.30 a.m. until 1 a.m., with free WiFi and a new, super quick and tasty burger, bagel, pizza and salad menu, Soho Theatre Bar is the perfect place to meet, eat and drink before and after our shows.

SOHO THEATRE ONLINE
Giving you the latest information and previews of upcoming shows, Soho Theatre can be found on Facebook, Twitter and YouTube as well as at sohotheatre.com.

HIRING THE THEATRE
An ideal venue for a variety of events, we have a range of spaces available for hire in the heart of the West End. Meetings, conferences, parties, civil ceremonies, rehearsed readings and showcases with support from our professional theatre team to assist in your events' success. For more information, please see our website sohotheatre.com/hires or to hire space at Soho Theatre, email hires@sohotheatre.com and to book an event in Soho Theatre Bar, email sohotheatrebar@sohotheatre.com

Soho Theatre is supported by Arts Council England and Westminster City Council.

Registered Charity No: 267234

Soho Theatre, 21 Dean Street, London W1D 3NE
sohotheatre.com
Admin 020 7287 5060
Box Office 020 7478 0100

THANK YOU

We are immensely grateful to our fantastic Soho Theatre Friends and Supporters. Soho Theatre is supported by Arts Council England and Westminster City Council. This Theatre has the support of the Pearson Playwrights' Scheme sponsored by Pearson plc.

Principal Supporters
Nicholas Allott
Jimmy Carr
Jack and Linda Keenan
Amelia and Neil Mendoza
Lady Susie Sainsbury
Carolyn Ward
Jennifer and Roger Wingate

Corporate Sponsors
Baites Wells & Braithwaite
Cameron Mackintosh Ltd
Caprice Holdings Ltd
Dusthouse
Financial Express
Fosters
Granta
The Groucho Club
Hall & Partners
Latham & Watkins LLP
Left Bank Pictures
Nexo
Oberon Books Ltd
Overbury Leisure
Ptarmigan Media
Quo Vadis
Seabright Productions Ltd
Soho Estates
Soundcraft
SSE Audio Group

Trusts & Foundations
The Andor Charitable Trust
Austin & Hope Pilkington Trust
Backstage Trust
Boris Karloff Charitable Foundation
Bruce Wake Charitable Trust
The Charles Rifkind and Jonathan
Levy Charitable Settlement
City Bridge Trust
The Coutts Charitable Trust
The David and Elaine Potter
Foundation
The D'Oyly Carte Charitable Trust
The Edward Harvist Trust
The Earmark Trust
The 8th Earl of Sandwich
Memorial Trust
The Eranda Foundation
Equity Charitable Trust
The Fenton Arts Trust
The Foundation for Sport
and the Arts
The Goldsmiths' Company
Harold Hyam Wingate Foundation
Hyde Park Place Estate Charity
John Ellerman Foundation
John Lewis Oxford Street
Community Matters Scheme
John Lyon's Charity
The John Thaw Foundation
JP Getty Jnr Charitable Trust

The Kobler Trust
The Mackintosh Foundation
The Mohamed S. Farsi Foundation
The Rose Foundation
Rotary Club of Westminster East
The Royal Victoria Hall Foundation
Sir Siegmund Warburg's
Voluntary Settlement
St Giles-in-the-Fields and William
Shelton Educational Charity
The St James's Piccadilly Charity
Teale Charitable Trust
The Theatres Trust
The Thistle Trust

Soho Theatre Best Friends
Johan and Paris Christofferson
Dominic Collier
Richard Collins
Miranda Curtis
David Day
Cherry and Rob Dickins
Wendy Fisher
Hedley and Fiona Goldberg
Norma Heyman
Isobel and Michael Holland
Beatrice Hollond
Lady Caroline Mactaggart
Christina Minter
Jesper Neilsen and Hannah
Seogaard-Christensen
Rajasana Otiende
Suzanne Pirret
Amy Ricker
Ian Ritchie and Jocelyne
van den Bossche
Ann Stanton
Alex Vogel
Garry Watts
Matthew and Sian Westerman
Hilary and Stuart Williams

Soho Theatre Dear Friends
Natalie Bakova
Quentin Bargate
Norman Bragg
Neil and Sarah Brener
Roddy Campbell
Caroline and Colin Church
Giles Fernando
Jonathan Glanz
Geri Halliwell
Anya Hindmarch and James
Seymour
Shappi Khorsandi
Jeremy King
Lynne Kirwin
Michael Kunz
James and Margaret Lancaster
Anita and Brook Land
Nick Mason
Annette Lynton Mason

Andrew and Jane McManus
Mr and Mrs Roger Myddelton
Karim Nabih
James Nicola
Phil and Jane Radcliff
Sir Tim Rice
Sue Robertson
Nigel Wells
Andrea Wong
Matt Woodford
Christopher Yu

Soho Theatre Good Friends
Oladipo Agboluaje
Jed Aukin
Jonathan and Amanda Baines
Mike Baxter
Valerie Blin
Jon Briggs
David Brooks
Rajan Brotia
Mathew Burkitt
Chris Carter
Benet Catty
Jeremy Conway
Sharon Eva Degen
Geoffrey and Janet Eagland
Gail and Michael Flesch
Sue Fletcher
Daniel and Joanna Friel
Stephen Garrett, Kudos Films
Alban Gordon
Martin Green
Doug Hawkins
Tom Hawkins
Anthony Hawser
Thomas Hawtin
Nicola Hopkinson
Etan Ilfeld
Jennifer Jacobs
Steve Kavanagh
Pete Kelly
David King
Lorna Klimt
David and Linda Lakhdhir
James Levison
Amanda Mason
Ryan Miller
Catherine Nendick
Martin Ogden
Alan Pardoe
David Pelham
Andrew Perkins
Andrew Powell
Geraint Rogers
Barry Serjent
Nigel Silby
Lesley Symons
Dr Sean White
Liz Young

We would also like to thank those supporters who wish to stay anonymous as well as all of our Soho Theatre Friends.

Supported using public funding by
ARTS COUNCIL ENGLAND
LOTTERY FUNDED

Supported by
City of Westminster

the Albany

Based in the heart of Deptford, the Albany is South East London's leading performing arts venue, with a history stretching back to the nineteenth century.

'The Albany is reaching out to local and wider audiences with its bold experimental programme.' *Time Out*

The Albany is building a strong reputation as a home and seeding ground for creative development in the arts. With four performance spaces, including a unique central performance space, our programme includes a range of theatre, music, circus, dance and spoken word, as well as an array of participatory projects.

We attract over 130,000 visitors a year, including 28,000 people attending performances and a further 40,000 taking part in workshops, events and creative projects. The Albany is home to 21 resident organisations and works in partnership with 200 community-based groups every year.

Recently, the Albany formed innovative partnerships with Lewisham and Southwark Councils to manage two new buildings housing libraries alongside cultural facilities – the Deptford Lounge and the Canada Water Culture Space – through which we have engaged more than 180,000 people.

2012 marked the Albany's 30th birthday on Douglas Way, with celebrations taking place until May 2013. For more information about our history and how you can get involved, please visit our website.

SENIOR STAFF
Chief Executive **Gavin Barlow**
Administrative Director **Senay Gaul** | Head of Operations **Fiona Greenhill**
Head of Creative Programmes **Raidene Carter**
Head of Business Development **David Johnson**
Head of Finance **David Lewis** | Head of Fundraising **Elizabeth Knock**
Marketing Manager **Rhian Hughes** | Box Office Manager **Vicky Harrison**
Operations Manager **Kate Miners** | Technical Manager **Ben Wallace**

The Albany
Douglas Way, Deptford, London SE8 4AG
020 8692 4446 | boxoffice@thealbany.org.uk
www.thealbany.org.uk

The Albany is grateful for the support of London Borough of Lewisham and Arts Council England.

Registered Charity no. 1112521

Lewisham

LOTTERY FUNDED | Supported using public funding by **ARTS COUNCIL ENGLAND**

GOD'S PROPERTY

Arinze Kene

Characters

ONOCHIE, *mixed-race, mid-teens, skinhead, dressed in 1980s skinhead fashion, tall and skinny, long-sleeve button-up Ben Sherman shirt, tight Lee jeans worn deliberately short to show off his burgundy socks and Dr. Martens boots, and black braces (suspenders)*

CHIMA, *his older brother, mixed-race, tall and brawny, late twenties, small afro, light-blue sports shirt, clean blue jeans, plain white tennis shoes*

HOLLY, *white, mid-teens, girl skinhead (skingirl), three-quarter-length jacket and matching miniskirt, fishnet stockings*

LIAM, *white, late twenties, short and stocky, large pronounced sideburns, a white vest, pyjama bottoms or boxers, trainers or boots or slippers*

Setting

1982, Deptford, South London.

All five scenes take place on the same set: a kitchen of a small council house in Deptford. The kitchen consists of a sink, upstage-centre, surrounded by counter space, a wall telephone, cupboards and a window with curtains above the sink. Stove. Refrigerator. Ceiling fan. A small wooden breakfast table with two matching chairs set across from each other. Stage-left there is a door opening to the back of the house.

Note On Sound

The sense of a growing number of dogs should be felt in the background, particularly in Scenes Four and Five.

Note On the Text

A forward slash (/) in the text indicates the point at which the next speaker interrupts.

This text went to press before the end of rehearsals and so may differ slightly from the play as performed.

Scene One

Lights up...

18:20

The kitchen.

Beat.

A hooded, shifty-looking figure appears at the back door. We cannot see the face of this person. The person looks into the kitchen through the window for a moment before... attempting to unlock the door. They have to try a few keys before the door swings open and they enter. It is a man. He brings in with him two big cargo bags. He places the bags down and takes off his large coat. We see him properly now. This is –

CHIMA. *He looks around. His appearance is unkempt and scruffy – suggesting that he has been sleeping rough. There is the sound of a dog barking outside – he looks over his shoulder and realises the door is still open. He goes and shuts the back door gently.*

Silence.

CHIMA (*calling out*). Mum?

He leaves the kitchen, walking around the house –

Mum!

You here? It's me.

We hear room doors open upstairs – then silence.

In that silence, ONOCHIE *arrives at the back door, a guitar case on his back – he finds it odd that the door is unlocked already. He enters and immediately freezes, looking with suspicion at the two cargo bags on the floor and the large coat on the table. The door slams shut behind him and –*

That you?

ONOCHIE *becomes unsettled upon hearing* CHIMA*'s voice and movements upstairs – the sound of somebody coming down.* ONOCHIE *quickly flips his guitar off his back. He reaches into his boot, pulls out a flick knife. He flicks it open and nervously holds it out just as* CHIMA *enters the kitchen.*

Beat. CHIMA *and* ONOCHIE *lock eyes with each other, both frozen.*

(*The top of this scene is done on the move as* CHIMA *is trying to elude* ONOCHIE*'s knife by going around the table.*)

Beat.

Ay.

ONOCHIE. Ay.

CHIMA. Ay.

ONOCHIE. Come on then!

CHIMA. Look.

ONOCHIE. Move!

CHIMA. I.

ONOCHIE. Move…

CHIMA. Listen –

ONOCHIE. Move back.

CHIMA. I'm…

ONOCHIE. Step back.

CHIMA. Stepping…

ONOCHIE. Back.

CHIMA. Stepping back look.

ONOCHIE. I'll…

CHIMA. Please –

ONOCHIE. I'll do it yer.

CHIMA. Put –

ONOCHIE. Explain.

CHIMA. Put that –

ONOCHIE. What the fuck –

CHIMA. Put it down.

ONOCHIE. Explain what the fuck –

CHIMA. Am I doing here?

ONOCHIE. Upstair!

CHIMA. I was looking –

ONOCHIE. Yer shouldn't 'ave been.

CHIMA. No, listen, I was looking for –

ONOCHIE. Yer nicking stuff – (*Kicks* CHIMA*'s bag.*)

CHIMA. Nah, this is my –

ONOCHIE. Yer what?

CHIMA. House.

ONOCHIE. Yer…

CHIMA. House.

ONOCHIE. Not possible.

CHIMA. Yeah.

ONOCHIE. Well, that's…

CHIMA. The truth.

ONOCHIE. The wrong answer, mate.

CHIMA. 14 Eddon Street.

ONOCHIE. Where *I* live.

CHIMA. Me too.

ONOCHIE. Yer…

CHIMA. Yes.

ONOCHIE. Yer obviously…

CHIMA. Got a bedroom upstairs.

ONOCHIE. Yer obviously wanna catch a stabbing.

CHIMA. Ono, listen.

ONOCHIE. WHAT?

CHIMA. Onochie.

ONOCHIE. Who the fuck...

CHIMA. See –

ONOCHIE. Who are yer?

CHIMA. I know your name cos –

ONOCHIE. HOW?

CHIMA. It's me.

ONOCHIE. Don't...

CHIMA. Please –

ONOCHIE. If yer move –

CHIMA. But you're –

ONOCHIE. Stop mo–

CHIMA. You got a knife at me.

ONOCHIE. Stop shuffling around then.

CHIMA. Okay!

ONOCHIE. OKAY!

CHIMA. Just. Now. Just.

ONOCHIE. Stab.

CHIMA. No need.

ONOCHIE. I will.

CHIMA. There is no need for that.

ONOCHIE (*suddenly panicking*). Fuck! Fuck.

     Where's –

CHIMA. Calm down.

ONOCHIE. She.

   She were 'ere before I left.

CHIMA. That's. That's what I'm trying to –

ONOCHIE. Where is…

CHIMA. It's why I was upstairs…

ONOCHIE. She's upstair –

CHIMA. I don't think she's here…

ONOCHIE. Where did she go?

CHIMA. Well, I just got in so I didn't catch her leaving –

ONOCHIE. She fuckin' here or not!

CHIMA. She ain't here I said –

ONOCHIE. Wait-wait-wait did yer…

CHIMA. No.

ONOCHIE. Yer 'urt 'er?

CHIMA. Course I never!

ONOCHIE. Yer went up and did what to 'er – I'll kill yer –

CHIMA. She's… behind you, look.

   ONOCHIE *looks over his shoulder and in that moment*
   CHIMA *skilfully disarms him and now has the knife*
   (CHIMA *could have him if he wanted to*). *Beat, as*
   ONOCHIE *looks at* CHIMA *then back at his own empty*
   hand.

ONOCHIE. Thass not funny.

CHIMA. Nah.

ONOCHIE. Give it here.

CHIMA. Ono, please –

ONOCHIE. Suit yerself.

ONOCHIE *grabs a kitchen knife out of a drawer – they're now both holding up knives, walking around.* ONOCHIE *comes lunging at* CHIMA *more aggressively now.*

CHIMA. OI!

ONOCHIE. Yer think I won't do yer –

CHIMA. Let's stop this.

ONOCHIE. THEN TELL ME WHERE SHE IS!

CHIMA. It's me. Chim.

ONOCHIE. Jim?

CHIMA. Chima.

ONOCHIE. Chima?!

CHIMA. Yes.

ONOCHIE. No, 'e's, uh…

CHIMA. It's me, Ono.

ONOCHIE. Do I look like some –

CHIMA. It's me.

ONOCHIE. Some prick.

CHIMA. Chima.

ONOCHIE. Nah.

CHIMA. Your brother.

ONOCHIE. Ma brother, is it?

CHIMA. Yes.

ONOCHIE. Yer juss…

CHIMA. Yes.

ONOCHIE. Yer juss beggin' to get stab now.

CHIMA. Nah.

ONOCHIE. 'Oo else…

CHIMA. Just me.

ONOCHIE. ...In my 'ouse.

CHIMA. I'm alone.

ONOCHIE. Fuckin'...

CHIMA. Chima.

ONOCHIE. Yer ain't...

CHIMA. Bro, listen –

ONOCHIE. Yer ain't 'im!

CHIMA. Look, I can prove –

ONOCHIE. TAKE –

CHIMA. Sorry.

ONOCHIE. YER 'ANDS OUT YER POCKETS!

CHIMA *slams his knife down onto the table.*

CHIMA. Fuck's sake, man, upstairs... the first door... that's my bedroom, yours is the second door, Mum's Irish, Dad's black, Nigerian, Dad was a – you were six years old, when he died, we uh, we used to go church when he was here, and uh you me and him would cook together, every Sunday, that was our thing. Onochie Chukwu Igwe is your full name, all down your leg you got a birthmark, goes all the way down, Mum says... she used to say it's cos she had an itchy leg when she was carrying you – Mum... Mum, don't like touching cardboard, said she hates the texture... she'd sing to us this made-up breakfast song when she cooked in the mornings: '*Eggy deggy...*' – we'd sit, around this table, the four of us... this is where Dad sat, you always were sat there, Mum would be the last to sit down every time as she'd have dished it all so she'd sit there, and that was my place...

I'm your brother.

It's me.

ONOCHIE *stares at him – still holding the knife up.*

(*Re: knife.*) Come on.

A moment, and then ONOCHIE *lets his arm come down. Shakes his head. Puts the kitchen knife away and takes his own off the table – he paces.*

ONOCHIE. 'Ow comes yer 'ere?

CHIMA. –

ONOCHIE. What yer 'ere for?

CHIMA *sits in his chair.*

Beat.

CHIMA. Sit down here with me for a sec.

ONOCHIE. Mum! Mum!

CHIMA. She ain't here –

ONOCHIE. Yer made her leave.

CHIMA. I didn't make her do anything.

ONOCHIE. Yeah yer did. Yer did cos she'd normally be 'ome this time.

CHIMA. Bro. Sit down.

ONOCHIE. She knew you were coming, didn't she? Cos that were you last week. Yer phoned up. Fuckin' knew it – that were you, weren't it? What'd yer say to 'er? Had 'er crying in the toilet afterwards. What 'ave yer done?

CHIMA. She was –

ONOCHIE. Leakin'. Cos of summit yer said.

CHIMA. Told her I'd be passing, that's all.

ONOCHIE (*pointed*). Well, that'll do it. To push her out the door, thass more than enough!

CHIMA. Ono, sit down a moment.

ONOCHIE. I'll sit down when yer fucked off, yer prick. Yer ain't welcome. She'd a' been upset with yer bein' 'ere! Yer made 'er walk out!

CHIMA. You're gonna change your tone of voice.

ONOCHIE. Do not threaten me!

You.

Do not.

Threaten.

Me!

Ain't 'fraid of yer.

CHIMA. Respect. Don't need you to 'fraid me just respect that I'm older –

ONOCHIE. Yer oughta know respect goes both ways – gimme that / older-brother shit…

CHIMA. You're foaming at the mouth – I've done nothing to you.

ONOCHIE. Yer in me 'ouse for one, / uninvited…

CHIMA. My house as much as it is yours.

ONOCHIE. Scared me mum off, she's already in a fragile state, now thanks to you, she could be out there crying, walking up an' down some bridge –

CHIMA. Don't say that –

ONOCHIE. Again! It's true. Yer ain' done enough already, yer wanna come back and finish 'er off. Fuck's sake.

CHIMA. –

ONOCHIE. Now, is that all what's 'appened?

CHIMA. Is what all what's happen–

ONOCHIE. What yer tellin' me, son, what yer just said.

That yer came and now she's gone.

Beat.

Yer even listening?! (*Checks* CHIMA*'s eyes.*) Hiding something. Yep. Fuckin' know it.

CHIMA *looks away.* ONOCHIE *reads this as him hiding something.*

(*Points his finger close to* CHIMA's *face.*) Look, more deceit.

CHIMA. You wanna get out of my face and calm down.

ONOCHIE *paces and boots* CHIMA's *bag.*

What did I just say?

ONOCHIE. It's what yer *not* saying!

ONOCHIE *boots* CHIMA's *bag again.*

CHIMA (*standing*). Do that again and see if I don't cancel your birth.

Beat.

ONOCHIE *looks at the bag. He walks to it and boots it again.* CHIMA *stares at* ONOCHIE – *he'd like to rip his head off but he sits back down at the table.*

You want it to be my fault.

ONOCHIE. Whose fault is it? Let's 'ave a twig at the math: yer show up outta nowhere, my mum suddenly up and leaves – you equal trouble.

CHIMA. That's what you reckon.

ONOCHIE. Thass what I know.

CHIMA. Well then, you don't know much, a lot, or a little bit.

ONOCHIE. I do know what's in yer nature. And obviously yer made 'er feel so uncomfortable in 'er own 'ome that she's 'ad to leave.

CHIMA. –

ONOCHIE. She don't want yer 'ere, man. Spelled it out to me a fuckin' trillion times, she don't like yer. Yer a disgrace, she says. 'Cording to her she only got the one son.

CHIMA. Yeah.

ONOCHIE. She's buried yer. Yer don't exist any more.

CHIMA. Did Mum *say* that – yes or no?

ONOCHIE. Says it all the time! Being honest 'ere, she's too nice to show yer forthright what she's truly thinking. *I* personally feel no way in relaying this to yer on the other 'and: she don't want yer 'ere. Say the neighbours see yer, then what? Yer thought 'bout that? They're only 'cross the road, for fuck's sake – yer fan club. Yer don't think, man. About what could happen. Yer comin' back 'ere, seriously, yer not right in yer 'ead.

CHIMA. You're my little brother. I wanted to see you, so I'm here, / what's wrong about that?

ONOCHIE. Why the hellfuck yer wanna see *me*, I don't know.

CHIMA. Haven't had connection with you in ten years – I'm not even complaining that you lot didn't come to visit me, not once. Know how that felt?! Other people, worst things they done, their families at least showed up for them once a year – wrote them, whatever.

ONOCHIE. Yer a grown man so I'll admit, setting down to write yer birthday cards dint cross me mind.

Lissen, we've nothin' in common but a surname. Other than that, what makes me connected to yer? Nothing.

CHIMA. –

ONOCHIE. Us to pretend everything's hunky-dory like yer dint do as yer done. We don't need yer sashaying through Deptford dressed in yer long humiliations, thank yer very much.

There's no way better sayin' this, no one wants yer round 'ere. No one. Yer only know deep down what it's gonna do to Mum – Is that it – that's yer intention? Cos yer going the right way about it.

Long beat.

CHIMA. She told me to look after you.

ONOCHIE. Mate. Do I... do I look like a pillock – yer just said she weren't 'ere when yer came.

CHIMA. When I phoned, when I told her I was coming, she said okay, she told me to look after you and yeah that's pillock's uniform you got on.

ONOCHIE. Why would she tell yer to look after me?

CHIMA. Said she wanted us to talk. And… thinking about it, maybe that's why she's not here. To give us some time alone. Catch up on each other. Make sense of all this.

Pause. ONOCHIE *shakes his head at this – he realises something.*

ONOCHIE. Fuck.

ONOCHIE *sits – something weighs heavy on his mind.*

CHIMA. We're brothers, Ono.

ONOCHIE. That is not relevant. She… she said all that to yer?

CHIMA. I wouldn't lie to you.

ONOCHIE. –

CHIMA. What.

ONOCHIE. Oh, it's nothing really, only that she's not said a word since last week. Since yer phoned that afternoon. Morning till night she's in bed. Won't say a word.

CHIMA. –

ONOCHIE. So let's, let's just backtrack, for a moment, rig the conversation that yer had with her, objectively: a depressive mother says to yer 'I need yer to look after my son.' And that don't sound odd to yer? No flag raised. It sounds normal to yer. It didn't sound at all a bit 'thank you goodnight'.

CHIMA. Didn't sound odd at the time.

ONOCHIE. How's it sounding now?

You've done this, ya know.

CHIMA. Mum's had issues.

ONOCHIE. 'Mum's had issues'? Yer gonna stand there and say Mum had issues?

CHIMA. She did –

ONOCHIE. She had issues because she had you! Yer the fuckin' issues, Chima! Really… yer summit else. Yer summit else altogether.

Left Mum to do all the cleanin' up of yer shit and yer have the guts to imply she's brought it on 'erself? She's gone through hell cos of yer. We've 'ad to take it from all the lot 'round 'ere. Been humiliated. It's all died down now thanks to me but we can't 'ave yer bring the trouble back to this 'ouse – This ain' a prodigal-son thing where yer return 'ome an' we give yer some big celebration, huge feast with an assortment of meats an' fish, nah. Yer must've 'ad yer legs crossed when yer made that wish. So excuse me if I don't leap at the opportunity to 'bond' with yer. The damage is irreparable, son. Yer can't spit back the chunk of flesh that yer tore out of this family.

ONOCHIE *goes to the door and opens it wide –*

I say yer'll 'ave to leave.

Grab yer shit, sling yer hook, yer gonna 'ave to get off. Let the door 'it yer where the dog shoulda bit yer.

CHIMA. You know what's out there for me.

ONOCHIE. Not my problem. Yer just come from out there to get 'ere so yer taken the risk already.

CHIMA. You don't care what happens to me.

ONOCHIE. Son, I'll tell yer what I do care about – I care about me mum. I care about strangers, in me 'ome, upsetting me mum. Man of the 'ouse? Me. Gotta protect 'er. So let's go, I can't leave yer in 'ere alone case she comes back and finds yer poncin'.

CHIMA *doesn't move.*

Look. Yer know that yer ain't entitled to be 'ere. She'll die of shame. Tell yer what, when I find 'er, I'll tell 'er yer said yer never meant to scare 'er off. What's more, Chim, I'll tell 'er that yer said yer sorry. Which is what yer never did say, Chim. Not to me, not to my mum… poor Sylvia, Old

Graham and Liam across the way, they ain't had a sorry out of yer. Never showed any remorse. Up till now. But I'll tell 'er that yer did. How's that?

Beat. CHIMA *nods. He starts to go to his bag on the floor –*

Good, man.

But CHIMA *begins bringing groceries and other foods out of the bag and putting them on the table. He looks to* ONOCHIE.

CHIMA. You're angry. I haven't been here for you and Mum. Okay. I'm here now. I walked all the way here. I've had to make my bed in a stairwell the last couple nights. I have not been smiling these past ten years. I haven't had pleasure from all this badness and discord. I ask that you please just for one moment think back to when we were okay. My best memory of us as a family is when you, Dad and me would cook on Sundays. Proper Nigerian food. You used to love that. If you can give me that, and let me clean myself up good and proper, rest my head on my pillow for a while… I'd be grateful. That's all I ask. What I am saying is that there are two types of pain you can feel here, little brother. The pain of putting up with me, for a little while. Or the pain of regret, that is everlasting. That you wear *under* your skin. Speaking from experience.

Silence.

ONOCHIE. The time is 18:50.

Yer sleep, shit, shower, shave, eat, drink, whatever. I'll give yer till dark, as it'll be less heated for yer walking through Deptford at that time. Yer get to stay 'ere until and not a minute after midnight. After that, yer gone – yer leave, yer don't come back. Thass me being generous. I won't be participating in any cooking of Nigerian food with yer this evening and nor will I be eating it. Yer just do yer thing and I'll do mine.

Agree to that.

Beat.

CHIMA *nods.*

Once it hits twelve yer gotta be out 'ere like yer chariot's gonna pumpkin.

CHIMA *nods.*

Not a minute after.

CHIMA. Okay.

ONOCHIE. Yer see, I want for it to be crystal clear that I ain' bein' tough for nothin' –

CHIMA. I said okay.

ONOCHIE. No, lissen, lissen, Mum wouldn't want yer 'ere is all –

I 'ave to protect 'er.

Is what I 'ave to do.

CHIMA. You're doing a good job –

ONOCHIE. If I don't – yeah, I know I am – if I don't, no one else will.

CHIMA. Not arguing with you, you're right.

ONOCHIE. Yer fuckin' right, I'm right.

ONOCHIE *closes the back door.*

Silence.

CHIMA *stands. He turns on the kettle. He grabs two mugs and places them on the table.* ONOCHIE, *wagging his head 'no', replaces one of the mugs.*

When'd yer get out anyway?

CHIMA. Some days ago.

ONOCHIE. Yer know I weren' actually gonna stab yer.

CHIMA. Ay, I understand there's a lot of hatred towards me / cos of –

ONOCHIE. No no no. I don't hate yer, Chima. I don't know yer, mate. But don't expect me to love yer either, cos I don't know yer.

CHIMA. You're dressed like that for what?

ONOCHIE. Like 'ow?

CHIMA. Like a racist.

ONOCHIE. A skinhead.

It's a way of life.

CHIMA. I know what a skinhead is. Ten years ago this was me.

ONOCHIE. Dressed like a racist, as yer so put it.

CHIMA. Didn't know it at the time.

Wore stuff like what you're wearing right now. Bought mine from the Barch Lever on the high street there. Passed by it yesterday on my way to the market getting all this – (*Re: groceries.*) Somehow you're dressed exactly like the white mannequin in the shop window there.

ONOCHIE. What yer gettin' to?

CHIMA. The desire to camouflage. Just saying I wore that too. Thought it'd relieve some of the pressure with living round here. Wanted to fit in. Camouflage into my surroundings. Called myself a skinhead.

ONOCHIE. Well, I ain' doin' it for the fit-in if thass what yer underscorin' – yer do know completely nothin' about me.

CHIMA. 'Can't beat 'em, join 'em' mentality.

ONOCHIE. Not for me.

CHIMA. What'd you get out of it then?

ONOCHIE. Those questions leadin' to my judgement get no volley. Yer not one to judge –

CHIMA. I weren't judging –

ONOCHIE. Yer simply oughta avoid any sort of moral condemnation. Far as I'm concerned.

CHIMA. You know you're black, right?

ONOCHIE. I'm mix. Made in England.

CHIMA. Guessing you're in a gang.

ONOCHIE. Summit like that, yeah.

What's more, we're a band. I play the bass.

CHIMA. Carrying that blade.

ONOCHIE. Gotta protect ourselves.

CHIMA. It's unnecessary.

ONOCHIE. Oh, it's necessary.

CHIMA. Right, so you've had to stick it in a man.

ONOCHIE. Not yet.

CHIMA. Well then, it's not necessary to carry it, then, is it.

ONOCHIE. Mate, yer live on dry land but yer learnt how to swim. Carrying a blade is very much like knowing how to swim. Neither is 'necessary' until the moment they are crucial. Until that moment yer find yourself drowning or the moment –

CHIMA. That a skinhead wants to remove my black head.

ONOCHIE. We do get on with the blacks. It's the Pakis we don't like.

Beat.

CHIMA. Right. No blacks in your gang though.

ONOCHIE. Not one. Not a single one.

Pause.

CHIMA. Huh.

Beat.

CHIMA *has drawn the curtain to peep out.*

Liam. Still living cushty with his mum and dad?

ONOCHIE. Best they didn't know you were 'ere. Ya know what I mean? They look this way.

CHIMA *takes the hint and comes away from the curtain.*

CHIMA. I see Old Graham still does the cars.

ONOCHIE. Old Graham's summit like the Godfather a
Deptford. Story for yer: 'e 'ad the Mayor of Lewisham over
for tea askin' 'is 'elp when the Front were gonna march
through 'ere.

CHIMA. He's with the Front.

ONOCHIE. Nah, don't think so. Everyone lissens to 'im is all.
Thass 'im. Other than that, yeah, 'e's still pretty much day in,
day out bangin' on cars right outside 'is 'ome there – allegedly
– but he's got other business, sidelines, yer know 'im.

CHIMA. Right.

And, uh...

ONOCHIE. Sylvia – yeah, she's still there too. Mostly see her
walkin' with flowers every Sunday for Poppy's grave – she's
sad. But she's always been kind to Mum – always. Talkin' to
'er when no one else would. Comin' over 'ere sometimes.
Helpin' out. When times were 'ard – when they had asked
Mum to leave the hairdresser's. They'd talk for hours in 'ere,
Sylvia and Mum. Old Graham never likin' it though. 'E'd
stand out there on the pavement after a while an' ask to 'ave
'er back. Never coming inside.

CHIMA *takes it all in.*

CHIMA. They given you any trouble?

ONOCHIE. Little bit over the years cos of the bad blood yer
caused obviously but we're cosy now, juss cosy.

CHIMA. You're in their gang, yeah?

ONOCHIE. Not exactly. Liam's doing jobs with Old Graham,
sidelining or doing whatever business they got, I mean he's
yer age, ain't he. Doesn't bother with our lot all that much
really. Don't get me wrong, Liam and Old Graham are well
within their right to get me to do summit, they're the olders,
so obviously I'll have to do it. Yer gotta do as yer told till yer
earn yer stripes.

CHIMA *looks at his brother.*

What.

CHIMA....I'm just.

ONOCHIE. What.

CHIMA. I spoke exactly like you, man.

Pause.

Does Mum never tell you that –

ONOCHIE. We don't talk about yer.

Honest to God, yer not mentioned in this 'ouse.

CHIMA. So you like it round here.

ONOCHIE. There's nothing to dislike. Sound. I'm well
regarded. Been a man of my word so I've got a good rep.

CHIMA. You've been out of school, what, four months?

ONOCHIE (*shrugs*). Summit like that. Why.

CHIMA. Not working.

ONOCHIE. Yer implying it's by choice?

CHIMA. Not even.

ONOCHIE. Ain't poncin' if that's what yer think.

CHIMA. Course not. You're clever. Know what Dad used to call
you when you were little because you were so clever and
couldn't take a joke? He called you / headmaster.

ONOCHIE. Headmaster. I know. Not funny.

CHIMA. How'd you do for the O levels?

ONOCHIE. Highest of everyone in my year. Got 'em all. I'm
very intelligent.

CHIMA. Yet the pocket stay dry.

ONOCHIE. Sometimes that's the case.

CHIMA. Sometimes. (*Nods.*)

The friends.

ONOCHIE. What of 'em?

CHIMA. In your gang. Bet they're not as intelligent.

ONOCHIE. What's it matter?

CHIMA. Are they working?

ONOCHIE. Naturally, some of them drift into the family
business they got. The others... yeah, most of them – pretty
much working.

CHIMA. You've had interviews though.

ONOCHIE. Course. But there's a skill to those, ain't there.
Reckon I've flunked them all but I got a few more later in the
month –

CHIMA. Mum ever tell you the reason Dad got sacked? Dad.
Dad, worked at the Post Office for fourteen years. Not a
problem. Never late. Never any trouble. It was hot one day
and Dad had a nosebleed. He had a nosebleed. They didn't
like that he bled everywhere.

So they give him the sack and he drank himself to death.

Pause.

Take it you didn't make the riots then.

ONOCHIE. Last year? Not a single reason for me to have been
there – joinin' in the animal behaviour.

CHIMA. Brixton's on your doorstep.

ONOCHIE. So's the Curry Café on Deptford High Street but
yer won't find me there very often.

CHIMA. You should've been there.

ONOCHIE. For what?!

CHIMA. For what? For the New Cross Fire.

For standing against Operation Swamp.

Sus.

Then brothers dying in custody.

The unemployment for us.

Last ones hired, first ones fired.

Living in shitholes and under bridges.

For that sign graffitied on the wall at the top of our road which clearly says for all to see 'we kill the niggers' – that's what for.

ONOCHIE. Yer presentin' an argument that may well in itself be valid but see it's only got fuck-all to do with me –

CHIMA. You're black.

ONOCHIE. Fuck-all. And I'm half-caste.

CHIMA. So you don't care.

ONOCHIE. Not that I don't care, son, but none of that 'appened to me.

I don't live under a bridge. Those weren't my mates in the inferno. And if I'm correct, yer in yer prison cell durin' all of that, so what's with pickin' up other people's battles?

CHIMA. They're our people!

ONOCHIE. They ain't my people… / you're just looking for trouble.

CHIMA. You telling me you haven't been called a monkey / or seen it happen –

ONOCHIE. Nope. Not me. Not in Deptford.

CHIMA. King Kong.

ONOCHIE. No.

CHIMA. Sambo.

ONOCHIE. Nah.

CHIMA. Golliwog.

ONOCHIE. I'm mixed.

CHIMA. Choc ice.

ONOCHIE. I said no.

CHIMA. Spade.

ONOCHIE. No.

CHIMA. Nig-nog. Jungle-bunny.

ONOCHIE. Not to my face.

CHIMA. They were your age. Burnt alive. Targeted because of they're black.

ONOCHIE. I think it's sad what's happened to them. But so's what yer done. That was sad also. But the world keeps spinnin'. It got to.

Pause.

We sit in silence long enough an' the mice are gonna come out. They've been runnin' everywhere recently. Saw one on the countertop this mornin'. I came in, it didn't even move. Stood its ground. You seen 'em?

Pause.

CHIMA. Might've saw one near the fridge as I came in.

ONOCHIE. Yeah, I know that one very well, he's, er, dirt-brownish colour?

CHIMA. That's the one.

ONOCHIE. Saw 'im last night. Strollin' like 'e owns the tile. Next breed of mice.

CHIMA. Next breed.

ONOCHIE. They come 'ere an' scavenge off us. Can't juss sit 'ere an' let 'em take off us. Catch the mouse an' squash its 'ead.

Pause.

Yer obviously found the hiding place then.

CHIMA. What hiding place?

ONOCHIE. Under the milk tray? The spare key, man.

CHIMA. Didn't need it. Used my old one.

ONOCHIE. Ah, yer still…

CHIMA. Yeah – (*Goes to get some things out of his bag.*) got given back all the stuff I had on me at the time...

CHIMA *brings out his old possessions, showing them to* ONOCHIE –

Burnt the word 'skin' into my wallet, see –

ONOCHIE. What's this?

ONOCHIE *holds up a picture.* CHIMA *looks at it.*

CHIMA. That is a picture of Poppy.

Beat.

ONOCHIE. Carrying that around for...

ONOCHIE *puts the picture back down – he stands.*

If I don't hear from Mum by tomorrow... I'm gonna involve the police.

Beat.

ONOCHIE *is heading to the hallway.*

CHIMA. I saw you last night.

ONOCHIE *stops and turns to* CHIMA.

Was out checking the area, you know. Walking about and I saw you.

ONOCHIE *shrugs.*

Was kind of late.

ONOCHIE. So?

CHIMA. Where'd you go?

ONOCHIE. Meet me friend.

CHIMA. What d'you get up to?

ONOCHIE. Juss coastin'. Why?

CHIMA. Just asking.

Coastin', yeah?

ONOCHIE. Coastin'.

   Smokin'.

CHIMA. With your friends.

ONOCHIE. Friend. Singular.

CHIMA. Friend. Singular.

   Is friend singular a girl?

ONOCHIE. What d'yer think?

CHIMA. Go on, what's his name then?

ONOCHIE. Prick.

CHIMA. You like her?

ONOCHIE. Yer a soddin' police investigator?

CHIMA. D'you like her? All I'm asking.

ONOCHIE. She's okay.

CHIMA. 'She's okay', so you like her then.

ONOCHIE. She's okay. She'll do.

CHIMA. How d'you know her, she go to your school or what?

ONOCHIE. She wishes she came to my school. All over me.

CHIMA. Okay.

ONOCHIE. It's the bass though. Bass or drums – if yer playing one of those, yer sorted. They're masculine instruments but they're also fanny magnets. I mean, I knew 'er from before – she's a mate of a mate or whatever. Her and 'er girls come to our gigs all the time no matter how far we're playing. But she don't really talk to us, like. Just these little looks – women. We 'ad a gig at The Red Tavern and it was getting fully intense, like, the bird was watching me the whole performance through and I don't take my eyes off 'er either. We come off the stage. I got me bass in me 'and, a drink in the other, I down it in a mighty gulp and we start towards the door cos we gotta catch the last bus obviously – that's when she makes 'er move, through the middle, like, parting everyone in the crowd, Red Sea, walks right up to me before I can get my foot out the door, starts talkin', givin' me all the interest. Didn't even look at the others. Made me miss my bus. Walked 'er home, gentlemanly, like. Been walking 'er 'ome ever since, if yer get my vernacular.

CHIMA. You've just got it like that?

ONOCHIE. This is how I've got it. And sometimes we don't exactly go straight 'ome, if yer know what I'm saying.

CHIMA. I think I gather. Back-of-the-cinema kind of larking.

ONOCHIE. Nah, mate. She's a lady. Most times we juss stay out an'... well... you know... she... helps me, with... writing lyric.

CHIMA. What?

ONOCHIE. I don't actually sing, I mean, I play bass but our singer couldn't string five letter out the alphabet let alone pen a song. So I'm the one writing lyric all the time. She normally helps out.

CHIMA (*unimpressed*). You write lyrics together.

ONOCHIE. Well, she's handy with the metaphors so – (*Shrugs.*) we make a good team, yes.

CHIMA *can't believe what he's hearing, he stares at* ONOCHIE.

CHIMA. You like that?

ONOCHIE. Yeah. I'm coastin' with 'er an' she acts all cute an' the sort. She's mellow like that. We might puff a bit, but we don't need to – I only do it cos it helps with my wisdom tooth coming through but yeah. When I'm with her... yeah.

CHIMA. Okay. Sounds to me like she's the one who's gonna take it.

ONOCHIE. Take it. Take what?

CHIMA. Your virginity, son.

ONOCHIE. Fuck off.

CHIMA. No – (*Demonstrates fingering.*) ah? Boys your age, they don't meet up to write lyrics, they're all – (*Demonstrates fingering.*)

ONOCHIE. Yer don't know 'er, all right. So let's just. Park this one up. Put the handbrake on so it don't roll back into conversation. Leave it there.

CHIMA. *Whar.*

I see that look, man.

ONOCHIE. What yer on about?

CHIMA. That.

ONOCHIE. Give it a rest, Chim.

CHIMA. You really like this bird of prey.

ONOCHIE. I… Ha…. Chima, son –

CHIMA. You haven't fingered her yet cos you respect her too much, no big deal.

ONOCHIE. Did I say that? Don't think I did.

CHIMA. It's in your eyes though.

ONOCHIE. 'Ow can – yer just – are yer so disgustin'? Ay? Is this what yer like then?!

CHIMA. You're offended.

ONOCHIE. Can you tell?!

CHIMA. I'm your brother, if you can't talk to *me* about this –

ONOCHIE. It's private.

CHIMA. Okay –

ONOCHIE. Come off it.

CHIMA. I'm done –

ONOCHIE. Give it a rest.

Pryin' into my life.

CHIMA *chuckles to himself.*

Anyway.

If she comes back 'ere again tonight –

CHIMA. Here?

ONOCHIE. Yeah. If she comes back 'ere –

CHIMA. She from Deptford?

ONOCHIE. She certainly is.

CHIMA. So she's white.

ONOCHIE. No, she's Japanese. Course she's white.

CHIMA. She know who I am?

ONOCHIE. Find a person in Deptford who doesn't know who yer are. I don't mean this in the good way but yer become a legend.

CHIMA. What do they make of you and her?

ONOCHIE. It's nobody's business, is it.

CHIMA. So they don't know. Your gang, her friends. They don't know about you and her.

ONOCHIE (shrugs). Only by chance.

CHIMA. Really.

ONOCHIE. We ain' keepin' it a secret or nothin'. I juss haven't told anyone an' she juss hasn't told anyone either. There's nothing *to* tell. It's our business –

CHIMA. Yeah, be careful with that business.

ONOCHIE. Wow. Been out of prison five minutes and yer dishing advice.

CHIMA. You know what I mean.

ONOCHIE. Haven't the slightest.

CHIMA. Do you need me to break it down / for you?

ONOCHIE. Let's stop talkin' about this, shall we? I can feel yerself getting' on my nerves.

CHIMA. She's coming here for what then?

ONOCHIE. This is where I was getting before yer interruption. She's said she gotta give me a message.

CHIMA. What's that?

ONOCHIE. Well, I don't know yet, do I. I'll need yer to –

CHIMA. What time she coming?

ONOCHIE. Jesus – *If* she comes...

Can't have yer creaking the floorboards.

I'd appreciate if yer...

Beat.

CHIMA (*loaded*). Yeah, you got it.

ONOCHIE *is heading to the hallway.* CHIMA *stands –*

Ono. Don't have much but...

CHIMA *goes into his pocket. He brings out a ten-pound note and puts it on the table.*

Have that if you want.

ONOCHIE. Why.

CHIMA (*shrugs*). Older-brother thing. If you're popping out, get me a Panda Pop. Do what you like with the change.

ONOCHIE. Which flavour?

CHIMA. Any.

The brothers just stand there, looking at each other.

ONOCHIE. How was it?

CHIMA. Humbling.

ONOCHIE. Go on.

CHIMA. Nothing can prepare you for it. No matter how hard you are.

Silence.

This, eh.

This young guy. About your age. Comes through. He's fresh. He's still got the scent of innocence about him, only been there a week or whatever. Half-caste brother. Bit nervous. Now, when you come it's all about family – what family you're with – it's important. You understand – you gotta run with a unit, a gang or whatever.

ONOCHIE. Yeah.

CHIMA. So it's the main block and in this building, to put it simply, you got about a hundred and twenty, a hundred and thirty inmates. But the main two families are the whites and the blacks, right? The whites and the blacks – and they don't seem to like each other very much – similar to here in Deptford. Now, as I said, this half-caste brother, he's in the middle, half'n'half. He's smart though, he knows that he cannot be with both – he has to make a choice or that leaves him unprotected in there. You don't wanna be unprotected in there. Both families are looking at him like 'Where you gonna go, kid, where you gonna go?'

He gets familiar with these white guys –

ONOCHIE. Thass right.

CHIMA. In particular there's four of them he's knocking elbows with. They're always together – in the canteen, on the grounds, in study, in the chapel, everything, that's his little posse – they're all right – he cracks a smile for the first time since he's been inside. But see, every time this half-caste guy looks over his shoulder in the canteen, on the grounds, walking back to his cell, wherever, every time he looks over his shoulder, he seems to lock eyes with black guys from the other family, they're watching him. Shaking their head at him, no malice – it's just as though... they're disappointed. He doesn't know why, cos the way he sees it, he's both black *and* white. He can choose.

ONOCHIE. Exactly.

CHIMA. Who the fuck are they to...

ONOCHIE (*wagging his head*). Fuckin'...

CHIMA. You know?

So. Wet rainy afternoon. Out on the grounds playing footy is half-caste and his four chums. One of them loses control of the football and it rolls off the pitch. The ball goes straight to the blacks congregating in a group there by the bench. Half-caste is not intimidated by this. From where he stood, he says: 'Oi. Pass it 'ere.' Well, the big blackies – some of them with dreadlocks – they're amused by this. They laugh at him, like he's a child, and they absolutely do not pass him the ball. Half-caste walks over, still cocky, like. He bends to pick up the ball and by when he stands back up, what's he got? Towering over him, a black man. Black man says (*Thick Jamaican accent*):

'Dey'll let you know.'

Half-caste – 'You what?'

'Dey'll let you know how black you are, bwoy.'

ONOCHIE. The fuck is he talking about.

CHIMA. That's what point-five thinks. He walks away. And he dislikes them all the more because the one thing they've actually said to him, don't make no damn sense – he's sure now that he made the right decision picking the white family.

Now, there comes a point where this black dude – sorry, half-caste, becomes comfortable enough to feel like he can trust these white boys alone. Now, the companies are really long, you got about forty cells back to back. It's twenty then you've got the staircase in the middle, and then there's the other twenty, so that's forty – staircase at the end as well. Twenty cells, staircase, twenty cells, staircase. And then you've got tiers, right, you've got one tier and then a second tier on top of that and then a third floor, but at this time the third floor was closed for, I can't even remember, but they only had the two floors. Now, half-caste, his cell just happens to be on the second tier way-way at the back of the company, right at the back, he's at the end. So, like, if he comes out of his cell and makes a left, he's walking into a brick wall – do you understand? The only way from his cell if he wants to come down from the second tier is back to the front, and that

a long way – he'll be walking past twenty cells before he
reaches the first staircase. Now, his four white friends, they're
walking towards him nice and quiet, and they go up the
staircase, because half-caste is on the second tier, and he
thinks it's all love, but today, he's standing outside his cell
looking at them coming to him, he stands there, they approach
him. And one of the white boys pulls out a street knife. Not a
prison shank, a street knife that he flicks out. Quickly. And in
that manor they grab half-caste under his arm right here and
right here, and around his neck here. And they stab him three
times in the gut. And the one who's choking him is pulling
him around like a rag doll. Trying to – basically they're trying
to kill him. Somehow. Somehow! His fear gets him out of
their hold. He manages to push past these four guys. Now he's
leggin' it. He's on the second tier remember so to the middle,
he's got twenty cells he's got to run by before he'll get to the
staircase, the guys are chasing him. Stabbing him in the back,
stabbing him in the back, numerous, numerous times, he picks
up speed but they catch him and stab him again, it happens
quick, I'm telling it to you slow but, it was quick. And he's
bleeding so much because he's fighting for his life and he's
running. Now the first staircase, he realises that he can't turn
to go down there because if he slips! If he slips then he's
gonna get killed up for sure, it's too narrow, he can't make it.
So what does he do?

ONOCHIE. –

CHIMA. He decides to keep running all the way to the front,
    what else, there's no other option, that's where the other
    staircase is. So that's another twenty cells, and he goes, and
    they're still behind him, he's coming up to the second
    staircase but hear this, same problem as before. The boys are
    even closer to him now. He's still blazing it down that second
    tier. What he decides to do, before he reaches that second
    staircase, instead of chancing it and slipping and having
    them sink that knife into his neck, what he decides to do…
    he decides, to jump. He jumps. The officers watching, other
    inmates watching – and it's like time had stopped.
    Everyone's watching. It's like this brother is flying. And he
    lands. He lands, right in the arms of the black family. They

catch him. They all put their hands out and they catch him –
place him on his feet. Their hands all on him – to keep him
upright – he's lost a lot of blood and he's weak. Half-caste is
surrounded by these big black guys that he's feared all his
life. And they don't smell, they don't try and fuck him – all
the things that he thought from shit that he heard, nah,
they're peaceful. One of them smiles and says to him – 'Dey
let you know, right?' And half-caste nods, cos for the first
time he understands them. He understands them too well.

ONOCHIE. Did he die?

Beat.

CHIMA. Never see him again after that.

Probably finished his time elsewhere.

ONOCHIE *takes the tenner off the table and goes to leave.
He reaches the door and turns around to* CHIMA –

ONOCHIE. He failed the test.

CHIMA. Ah?

ONOCHIE. The fucka failed the test. When the football went
over to the blacks, his mates were testing him. He was meant
to do summit. Spit in the face of one of their majors or
summit. Let 'em know who's boss.

That's what I would've done.

CHIMA *watches* ONOCHIE *leave.*

CHIMA *then gets up – looks through the window and checks
that* ONOCHIE*'s gone. Then he gets something out of his
pocket – it's a note. He puts it on the table – he looks at it – it
bothers him – he looks back to the door where* ONOCHIE
*has just left. He comes back to the table and he picks the note
up – he reluctantly tears it into pieces.*

Lights to black.

Scene Two

21:40

The lights come up and we see –

HOLLY *and* ONOCHIE *in the kitchen.* (HOLLY *is savvy, quick-witted, and confident.*) ONOCHIE *has his bass guitar in his hand – it's not plugged in, but throughout the scene he might come back to it, practising the same riff melody – it can be heard a little – he plays the complete riff at perfect times in between/during dialogue.*

HOLLY *recites lyrics from a sheet of paper –*

HOLLY.
'In the centre of the saddest story,
Smiles and chuckles at the rules of hate,
We think we understand the rules of hate,
Until we find we're slamming on the brakes,
Screeching on towards the journey's end,
But you know you've changed your mind too late,
There has to be another outcome surely,
In the centre of the saddest story.'

Yeah… that's it.

Pause.

ONOCHIE *just nods.*

ONOCHIE. That's…

HOLLY. Yeah.

ONOCHIE. Okay – (*Nodding to himself.*) Okay…

HOLLY. What do yer –

ONOCHIE. Just –

HOLLY. Yer need a second –

ONOCHIE. To, erm… tally this one up, yeah. (*Nods to himself.*)

HOLLY. I mean –

ONOCHIE. It's obviously not –

HOLLY. Our usual sort of thing.

ONOCHIE. Not remotely close.

HOLLY. But what do yer think though?

ONOCHIE . I mean. It's dark, like. It's definitely dark, like. Which is, you know… I like it but yer didn't even let me –

HOLLY. Sorry.

ONOCHIE. Normally we write 'em together, don't we, twinkle.

HOLLY. I'm sorry.

ONOCHIE. What 'appened?

HOLLY. Didn't feel to write another love song is all.

ONOCHIE. Yer don't rate me lyric or what.

HOLLY. I do, I just… (*Shrugs.*)

ONOCHIE. Just saying I easily could've chipped in is all.

HOLLY. It all just came out.

ONOCHIE. It has, hasn't it?

HOLLY. Yeah. Sadly.

ONOCHIE. Yer written purely about hate, Holly.

What's inspired this?

HOLLY. It's more about forbidden love. Well…

ONOCHIE. There's another fella then.

HOLLY. Yer silly sod.

ONOCHIE. Won't stand for it – who is he?

HOLLY *smacks* ONOCHIE*'s arm.*

Had a pressie for yer at the ready as well.

HOLLY. For me?

ONOCHIE. Was gonna give it to yer when we finished writing together but seein' as we've not written together, being that yer just relieved me of my services –

HOLLY. Oh, I never –

ONOCHIE. I can't give 'em to yer now.

HOLLY. Yer teasing. Yer never got me anything. Did yer?

ONOCHIE. Yer been naughty, Holly.

HOLLY. Oh, go on.

ONOCHIE. It's yer favourites as well.

HOLLY. Give 'em to me.

ONOCHIE. But yer come to me with a song about hatred.

HOLLY. Forbidden love.

ONOCHIE. Same difference, either way it means I can't give yer this –

ONOCHIE *pulls a paper bag out of a cupboard – it's filled with something.*

HOLLY. What's in there?

ONOCHIE. Have to bin it now.

ONOCHIE *holds it over the bin –* HOLLY *jumps up –*

HOLLY. No! Please, all right, I'm sorry – what did yer wanna write about?

ONOCHIE *is still holding the bag over the bin.*

ONOCHIE. Doesn't matter now, does it – (*Goes to drop it in the bin.*)

HOLLY. Okay! Next time, I let yer take lead. We write about whatever yer want.

ONOCHIE. Whatever, yeah?

HOLLY. Within reason, yes.

ONOCHIE *goes to drop the bag in the bin again –*

Okay, whatever. Whatever yer want.

ONOCHIE. Even if I wanna write about – (*Feigning thought.*) ptshh, I don't know – sex?

HOLLY. What yer wanna write about that for?

ONOCHIE. Yes or no.

HOLLY. Well, I don't know anything about sex.

ONOCHIE (*enticingly*). Nor do I.

> HOLLY *looks at him funny.*

HOLLY. Mate. We'll write about whatever yer want. Just gimme my pressie.

> ONOCHIE *walks over to* HOLLY *and empties the bag out on the table – falling out of the bag is an impressive range of pick'n'mix sweets, the bag was filled with them, a few bags of crisps too –* HOLLY *screams!*

ONOCHIE. Calm down.

> HOLLY *scoops the mountain of sweets up in her arms and lets them fall again –*

HOLLY. Oh my God! Ono!

ONOCHIE (*getting sodas from the fridge*). Got Panda Pops as well –

HOLLY. Heaven. All for me –

ONOCHIE. Do not touch the white mice –

HOLLY. They're nasty anyway.

ONOCHIE. Well, they're mine.

HOLLY. Yer like yer *white* mice, don't yer?

ONOCHIE. Not as much as yer like yer *brown* cola bottles.

> ONOCHIE *sits on the table and* HOLLY *sits on the chair beside him and they stuff their faces with sweets – much of the rest of the scene plays out with them chewing on sweets and snapping long snakey sweets in half so as to share them.*

HOLLY. Mmm.

ONOCHIE. Holly, about this song, the boys are gonna ask me loads of questions.

HOLLY. Yeah.

ONOCHIE. I mean, they'll like it but. It never feels right, taking all the credit. Them lot patting me on the back with every new lyric when deep down I know yer the mastermind.

HOLLY. We've already spoken about this –

ONOCHIE. They're yer songs, treacle.

HOLLY. They can't know I've written it.

ONOCHIE. They won't mind. Promise. Just come to practice tomorrow evening and I'll tell 'em.

HOLLY (*firm*). No.

Beat. They continue eating the sweets –

ONOCHIE. Oi!

HOLLY. What.

ONOCHIE. Yer just had one of me white mice!

HOLLY. So, what yer gonna do?

ONOCHIE. Listen. Yer don't wanna try me on.

HOLLY (*pretending to be frightened*). Oh no, Ono. Or what?

ONOCHIE *puts on a playful 'evil kidnapping villain' act.*

ONOCHIE. Or I'll... I'll tie yer down / an' juss –

HOLLY. Tie me down with what, with what?

ONOCHIE. With erm... the telly wires.

HOLLY. Then what?

ONOCHIE. Then I'll... I'll...

HOLLY. Do evil things to me I hope.

ONOCHIE. Yes.

That. Is what I'll 'ave to do.

HOLLY. Evil things like what?

ONOCHIE. Like, well… I'll juss 'ave to kiss yer… on yer lip.

HOLLY. On my lip, juss the one then?

ONOCHIE. Lipsss, / lipsss.

HOLLY. Holy Fuckin' infernal Christ, thass so evil.

ONOCHIE. Yes.

HOLLY. Never knew yer 'ad that in yer, Ono boy, good man.

ONOCHIE. So don't push me.

HOLLY. Come again?

ONOCHIE. Don't push me –

HOLLY. Cos yer close to the edge? Are yer tryin' not to lose yer
head? Ah huh-huh-huh-huh.

ONOCHIE. I'll do it.

HOLLY. Yeah – bet yer won't.

ONOCHIE. Don't test me, woman.

HOLLY. Testin' testin' one, two, three.

ONOCHIE. Well then, yer leave me no choice.

*He approaches her slowly like an animal after its prey. He
knows he's meant to be confident with her, but he is quite shy
inside, he's trying his best.*

HOLLY. Fuckin' 'ell, I might die a natural cause before yer'll
arrive.

ONOCHIE *gets there, he kisses her – but* HOLLY *does most
of the kissing, cupping his face in her hands.*

A floorboard creaks upstairs and HOLLY *immediately pulls
away.*

Whass that noise? Lissen.

ONOCHIE. What –

HOLLY (*whispers*). Lissen.

ONOCHIE. It wasn't anything –

HOLLY. Shhhh.

They sit in silence, listening. HOLLY *breaks the silence by dipping her hand into her crisp packet.*

If I 'ear it again I'll tell yer.

ONOCHIE *looks out the window.*

My godfather out there?

ONOCHIE. Jeez. Why yer always gotta remind me he's yer blimmin' godfather all the time –

HOLLY. Cos he is –

ONOCHIE. Yer can't just call him Old Graham like everyone else.

HOLLY. He's me godfather, Ono.

ONOCHIE *looks out the curtain again.*

ONOCHIE. Reckon that's his feet under the Renault.

HOLLY. It ain' zackley gonna be spastic Liam – he don't know 'is ass from 'is elbow.

ONOCHIE. More often he's out there now. Feels like he's watching over. Saw him staring this way only yesterday afternoon.

HOLLY. What yer think he'll do if he knew I were in 'ere?

ONOCHIE *doesn't respond – he continues looking out –*

He probably knows, yer know.

ONOCHIE *moves away from the curtain, grabs his bass guitar again – sits – he plays a bit – something weighs heavy on his mind.* HOLLY *looks at him.*

Hear what I just said?

ONOCHIE. Liam summit…

HOLLY. Yer ain't all 'ere today, hun.

 ONOCHIE *is pensive.*

 Knock knock, anyone 'ome?

ONOCHIE. Ah?

HOLLY. Juss enquiring 'bout the disturbance upstairs?

ONOCHIE (*paranoid*). There's no one upstairs.

HOLLY (*taps his head*). In yer skull, yer pleb.

 Remember I wanted to tell yer something today?

 ONOCHIE *doesn't answer.*

 ONOCHIE *drags his chair closer to* HOLLY*'s and kisses her. Under the table,* ONOCHIE*'s hand runs up her knee, he runs it up her thigh, he gets close to her privates – she smacks his hand.*

ONOCHIE. Ow!

HOLLY. Yer fucka!

ONOCHIE. Wha'd I do?

HOLLY. Wha'd yer do? What did yer do!

 HOLLY *smacks him again.*

ONOCHIE. Didn't even gimme a warnin', like.

HOLLY. Thass yer warnin'. First an' final.

ONOCHIE. So I can't touch yer then?

HOLLY. No. Not there please.

ONOCHIE. Why not?

HOLLY. Why all of a sudden yer wanna touch me down there for? Why?

ONOCHIE. Because.

HOLLY. What's it gonna do for yer?

ONOCHIE. Ah?

HOLLY. What yer gonna gain?

ONOCHIE. I dunno.

I juss wanna feel it.

HOLLY. 'E juss wanna feel it, 'e says. Well, that makes it all
right.

ONOCHIE. Honestly I think 'bout feelin' it all the time now,
it's ridiculous.

HOLLY. Well then, yer not okay any more, hun. Yer not well.

ONOCHIE. It's the next level.

HOLLY. What next frickin' level?

ONOCHIE. The next one.

HOLLY. No one informed *me* 'bout these levels. Where were I?

ONOCHIE. We're on the first level still. For ages now we been
'ere. I've explored every room on this floor. Next level, level
two, is where I'm tryin' to take us. Third level is the boom-
pow, but I ain' even askin' that right now.

Pause.

HOLLY *looks at him like he's crazy.*

HOLLY. Who yer been talkin' to?

ONOCHIE. No one.

HOLLY. Oh my God. That's what all this is for! The sweets, the
crisps –

ONOCHIE. Not exactly –

HOLLY. Yer trying to sweeten me up so I'd let yer molest me.

ONOCHIE. We've been kissin' for ages, Holly.

HOLLY. There's not a thing wrong wi' kissin'.

ONOCHIE. I need the next level. The way I feel, something like
a crab thass outgrown 'is shell, Holly. Juss let me stroke yer
fanny.

HOLLY. Oh my gosh? (*Moves further back.*) Don't call it that!

ONOCHIE (*laughing, teasing her*). Fanny!

He playfully chases her around the kitchen.

HOLLY (*slaps his arm*). Stop bein' nasty-ERR! Whass gotten into yer?

ONOCHIE. Nothin'.

HOLLY. Yer dirty perverted boy. (*Softly, playfully slaps his face.*) Look at yer glassy eyes, yer so horny.

ONOCHIE. I'll let yer feel me cock if yer –

HOLLY. NOOO!!!!!!! NOOOOO!!!

ONOCHIE. O-kay. Calm down. (*Offended a little.*) Fuckin' 'ell, what's wrong with my cock?

HOLLY. When I leave yer can feel yer cock well into the night, mate.

ONOCHIE. But I wanna feel yer fanny.

HOLLY. Wha–

HOLLY *raises her hand to beat him. He flinches.*

…wha'd I juss say?! Stop comin' near us.

ONOCHIE. What d'yer want me to call it 'en?

HOLLY. Don't call it.

ONOCHIE. Yer vagina.

HOLLY. Fuckin' no.

ONOCHIE. What then –

HOLLY. I dunno!

Me mum calls it 'the flower'.

ONOCHIE. Hmm. That ain't such a good name, yer know.

HOLLY. Why's that?

ONOCHIE. Cos it makes yer think 'bout gettin' nectar from it.

HOLLY. No it doesn't!

ONOCHIE. In my 'ead it kinda does!

HOLLY. Cos yer got a horn on yer 'ead, yer flippin' rhino, only *you*. Filthy sick child. Why yer sweaty? God, yer too nasty – look at yer face.

ONOCHIE *is closing in on her by the sink* – HOLLY *is loving it.*

Go away!

ONOCHIE. May I touch yer flower, please?

HOLLY. Don't yer dare call it that! Me mum calls it that, yer want me to picture me old mum in 'er green apron every time?

ONOCHIE. I'll call it 'It'. Can I feel It?

HOLLY. Call it…

The Portfolio.

ONOCHIE. Yer fuckin' what?

HOLLY. Portfolio.

ONOCHIE. Know what…

Respectfully, Holly, can I extract some nectar from yer portfolio?

HOLLY *is blushing now.*

Is what I think is 'appening 'appening?

HOLLY *smiles uncontrollably.*

An' she's doin' it! Oooh!

She quickly covers her face with her hands.

(*Teasing her, loving it.*) The shyness! It's the shyness!

HOLLY (*covering her face*). Yer can't! I won't let yer.

ONOCHIE. Aww, yer sooo cute when yer shy, yer know that? I love yer – it. I love it. When yer blushin'.

HOLLY (*speaking through her hand*). Yer can't touch me there, okay? Yer can feel yer own fanny instead.

ONOCHIE (*trying to peel back her fingers*). I beg yer, let me see the smilin' lips amid the shyness face.

HOLLY. Yer even listenin'? Said yer can't molest me down there.

ONOCHIE. Okay okay, juss show me the smile, love yer smile, I'll settle for the smile.

HOLLY. Yer can't feel it, okay?

ONOCHIE. Jeez, I said fine, babe, all right. Now, the smile.

HOLLY (*still covering face*). So... yer don't wanna touch me down there any more?

ONOCHIE. No.

Promise.

HOLLY. Why not?

ONOCHIE. What'd yer mean, 'Why not' –

HOLLY. D'yer think I'm scuzzy down there?

ONOCHIE. Scuzzy – Nah, yer –

HOLLY. Then 'ow come yer don't wanna touch me?

ONOCHIE. I do, / but yer –

HOLLY. Yer juss said yourself that yer didn't!

ONOCHIE. I tried, an' yer severed me arm!

HOLLY. Cos yer don't know what yer gettin' self into!

ONOCHIE. Sweet pea, yer hardly making any sense – do yer wanna go to the next level or not?

HOLLY. When yer gonna shut up about these levels?

ONOCHIE. When we're on level two.

Pause.

HOLLY (*a realisation to herself*). I can't. I can't – / what am I doing…

ONOCHIE. Yer can't what –

HOLLY. It's complicated.

ONOCHIE. Twinkle?

HOLLY. It's so complicated, Ono.

ONOCHIE. Go on. Let's speak on it.

HOLLY. I…

ONOCHIE. We tell each other everything. No secrets.

HOLLY. –

ONOCHIE. Make me understand.

HOLLY. Make yer understand.

ONOCHIE. Yeah.

    HOLLY *concedes.*

HOLLY (*reluctantly*). Okay, we're on level one…

ONOCHIE. Now she's talkin' –

HOLLY. Obviously the only way to get to level two, is up the stairs…

ONOCHIE (*begging her*). THASS! Thass what I been sayin' to yer, let's go up, I'm ready –

HOLLY. I'm gonna punch yer in the mouth in a minute, I will.

    The only way to the next level is up the stairs.

ONOCHIE. You know this.

HOLLY. And I do wanna go with yer but… (*Demonstrates pushing imaginary wheels on the chair she's sitting in.*)

    Wheelchair.

    I'm in a wheelchair, Ono.

ONOCHIE. Let me carry yer.

HOLLY. Yer not strong enough.

ONOCHIE (*getting out the chair*). Wanna bet?

HOLLY. Don't –

ONOCHIE *picks her up and has her in his arms.*

ONOCHIE. See?

He kisses her. He starts spinning her around.

Easy, look.

It's sweet but HOLLY *jumps off him and sits back down again – frustrated.*

Twinkle-toes, yer breaking my heart.

ONOCHIE *sits near her. He kisses her. They start snogging. He tries again – running his hand up her thigh. She smacks his hand then covers her face back up again.*

Ow?! Give up – / I give up.

HOLLY. We 'ave to talk 'bout something.

ONOCHIE. Nah, s'all right, Holly. I don't wanna do it ne'more.

HOLLY. YES YOU FUCKIN' DO, NOW SIT YOUR BLACK ARSE DOWN!

Silence.

HOLLY *points to the chair.*

ONOCHIE *sits.*

We really should talk about the song, Ono...

ONOCHIE. Don't wanna talk about the song.

Why can't we go to level two?

HOLLY. Cos.

ONOCHIE. Cos...

HOLLY. Well, for one I'm not even yer girlfriend, but –

ONOCHIE. Why not?

HOLLY. Yer ain' asked me yet, yer pillock, but that's not –

ONOCHIE. Thass why, yeah?

HOLLY (*sighs*). It's one of the reasons… but mainly it's… some other stuff…

ONOCHIE. What if I make yer my girl?

HOLLY *shrugs*.

Would yer even *wanna* be?

HOLLY *shrugs*.

Yeah yer do. Cos yer don't wanna hear 'bout me splashin' about. You'd be jealous.

HOLLY *is amused.*

Wanna keep me to yerself. Want the other birds to know to stay on their branch. Keep their claws off –

HOLLY. Other birds couldn't know. It'd be like now – if I were yer girlfriend it'd have to be our secret.

Pause.

ONOCHIE. Why's that then?

HOLLY. Yer know how they are.

ONOCHIE. What are they like?

HOLLY. They'll be funny.

ONOCHIE. Cos I'm a year older than yer.

HOLLY. Yeah and cos yer a black mainly.

ONOCHIE. But.

I'm more half-caste, aren't I, Hollz? Look –

ONOCHIE *puts his forearm with* HOLLY*'s forearm.*

Nearly as pale as yer.

HOLLY. Cos the family history then.

Pause. ONOCHIE *settles, deflated.*

ONOCHIE. There's nothing I can do about that, sweet pea.

HOLLY *strokes* ONOCHIE*'s face – she's burning inside.*

HOLLY (*sighs*). I know, love.

Holly Chukwu Igwe. Huh. Imagine that.

She kisses him. She takes ONOCHIE*'s hand and places it on her thigh. They kiss. His hand rises, disappearing up her skirt, she closes her eyes.*

(*Still kissing.*) Uhh –

ONOCHIE *fingers* HOLLY. *She puts her hand on his neck and he pulls his chair in closer so he can find her groove.* HOLLY *moans louder and stronger –* ONOCHIE *throws a look towards the kitchen door –*

ONOCHIE (*paranoid, to* HOLLY). Shhh.

HOLLY *abruptly pulls her chair away from him and stands.*

HOLLY (*backing up*). Fuck fuck fuck fuck fuck fuck fuck that were good, that felt too good – Ono. I'm so sorry. I'm sorry.

ONOCHIE. What yer sorry for?

HOLLY. FUUUUCK! AAAAH! (*Screams at the top of her lungs.*)

HOLLY *runs across the room – jumps onto the countertop.*

ONOCHIE. Whoa! Whass the matter?

HOLLY. What was that?!

ONOCHIE. What?!

HOLLY. Yer got things movin' in yer kitchen!

ONOCHIE. What?

HOLLY. I saw summit movin' over there in the corner, movin'.

She points near the fridge.

ONOCHIE. Nah.

HOLLY. Is it there?!

ONOCHIE. Calm down.

HOLLY. Ono, yer have small animals in yer kitchen!

ONOCHIE. Yer sure yer eyes ain' playin' tricks on yer?

We hear the sounds of someone coming down the stairs. This frightens HOLLY *even more.*

HOLLY. Aaah!! (*Screams.*) I can 'ear it!!

ONOCHIE. Calm down.

HOLLY. Stop tellin' me to calm down!

ONOCHIE. Well, yer overreacting!

CHIMA (*offstage*). Ono!

ONOCHIE. Shit.

HOLLY. Who was that?!

ONOCHIE. Thass...

CHIMA *rushes in, he tries to gauge the situation.*

HOLLY (*re:* CHIMA). Ono –

CHIMA. What's happened?

ONOCHIE. She reckons she saw summit –

HOLLY. I know I saw something! Saw a creature over there in the corner where yer standin', mister.

ONOCHIE. No yer didn't.

HOLLY. I did!

ONOCHIE. Her eye's playin' tricks on 'er.

CHIMA. This corner?

HOLLY. Yeah, thass the place.

ONOCHIE. How'd yer know for sure?

HOLLY. Cos I saw it wimme fuckin' eyes, yer idiot prick!!

CHIMA. Ah of course!

HOLLY (*getting frightened*). It's come back?

CHIMA. No no, there's a perfectly logical explanation for this. I'm looking after my mate's pet hamster for her while she's on holiday but yesterday Little Beefy escaped from his cage, you say you saw him in this area?

HOLLY (*holding back tears*). Yeah.

CHIMA. Good good. That means the neighbour's cat hasn't got to him, phew, I'd have been in big trouble – Hey don't cry, don't cry, he's just running around the house till he finds his way back to his cage, I assure you he's harmless.

HOLLY (*to* ONOCHIE, *crying*). Why yer didn't juss say!!

ONOCHIE. Cos yer were screamin' yer 'ead off –

CHIMA. He didn't know – Sorry, totally slipped my mind to tell you this morning.

HOLLY. Didn't even believe me.

ONOCHIE. Not that I didn't / believe yer –

HOLLY. YOU DIDN'T BELIEVE ME! So shut it!

CHIMA. We're okay, guys, we're okay. No need to get upset.

Now, come down from there, come down, let me – (*Helps her down.*) Look at you, you're shaking. Little Beefy is nothing to fret about, he 'fraids you more than you 'fraid him.

HOLLY *dries her eyes.* ONOCHIE *doesn't quite know what to say or do.* CHIMA *looks at them both.*

(*Looks at* ONOCHIE.) Hello, cousin.

Beat.

ONOCHIE. Holly, this is me cousin –

CHIMA. Linton – (*Puts his hand out to shake.*)

Beat as HOLLY *stares at* CHIMA.

HOLLY. Failed to mention yer cousin was here.

ONOCHIE. Yer never asked.

HOLLY. Pleasure to meet yer – (*Finally shakes his hand.*) Holiday.

CHIMA. Nice to meet you, Holiday.

HOLLY reverts her gaze to the area around the fridge again.

He's probably found a safe little hiding place somewhere – you've rattled him.

ONOCHIE. Yeah, Little Beefy's probably / hidin' some place...

HOLLY. Don't call him out, yer prat. / Are you such a prat? Honestly?

ONOCHIE. Wasn't calling 'im, yer mong!

HOLLY. Yer all callin' out 'is name – look at me, me 'ands still shakin' an' yer wanna set 'im on me again.

ONOCHIE. I were tryin' to be nice.

HOLLY. Nah, juss shut up, don't wanna 'ear it.

CHIMA. Guys, let's, cool down, ey?

HOLLY. I am cool, it's *this* moose.

Pause. CHIMA *is staring at* HOLLY. ONOCHIE *clears his throat and subtly gestures for* CHIMA *to leave them.* CHIMA *doesn't respond.*

ONOCHIE. Thank yer, Linton.

Beat – as CHIMA *remains where he is.*

Linton. Thank yer.

Pause.

CHIMA *looks at* ONOCHIE *now, then he goes to leave. However, he reaches the door and turns back to them once more –*

CHIMA. Look, all of this was my fault, let me make it up to you, Holly.

ONOCHIE (*chokes*). Ah? What'd yer...

CHIMA. I bought all this food earlier, haven't had the chance to cook it –

ONOCHIE. Sorry?

CHIMA. Ono's lost touch with his culture but I'll have you know he used to love cooking, it was like a ritual when his dad was around – you were quite good at it, weren't you, Ono?

ONOCHIE. No, mate. I'll see ya later.

Beat.

CHIMA. Holly, what do you say?

ONOCHIE. Very funny, Linton, off yer go now.

HOLLY (*sitting down*). Yeah, all right.

ONOCHIE. Nah, Holly's gotta be 'ome soon.

HOLLY. No I don't.

ONOCHIE. Yeah, yer do, Holly – Holly? Up yer get.

HOLLY. Ono, what's the matter with yer?

> ONOCHIE *doesn't know what to say.* CHIMA *starts getting ingredients out of the fridge.*

CHIMA. Hope you're hungry.

HOLLY. Yeah, I'm starvin' –

ONOCHIE. Yer juss eaten –

HOLLY. Crisps and sweets, thass not food.

ONOCHIE. Uh... Len... Linton –

CHIMA. Ono, if the girl wants to stay for some proper food, let her, be a gentleman.

HOLLY. Yeah.

Yer never feed me. He never feeds me properly.

> CHIMA *ploughs on – grabbing a knife out of the drawer.* ONOCHIE *doesn't approve – he also doesn't really know what his brother is playing at.*

CHIMA. You, uh, you had Nigerian food before?

HOLLY. Not that I know of.

Lights to black.

Scene Three

23:10

HOLLY, CHIMA *and* ONOCHIE *are at the table, the remnants of ẹbà and egusi soup on their plates, no cutlery.*

ONOCHIE *is in a bad mood – he's practising the same guitar riff again – he plays the complete riff at perfect times in between/during dialogue.*

HOLLY *gulps down some water – it seems she's having difficulty talking.*

HOLLY. Linton. That were. Actually. Really good.

ONOCHIE. Huh.

CHIMA. You think so?

HOLLY. It may have. Burnt my lips off but. I'm still. Well impressed.

CHIMA. I'm impressed you cleaned up plate. Ono, couldn't even finish.

ONOCHIE (*recriminating*). It ain't meant to be that hot.

CHIMA. You ain't had it in a while. He's just a lightweight. Can't take the heat.

   HOLLY *inhales and exhales quickly, trying to get cool air into her mouth.*

   (*Standing.*) You're really suffering, let me get you more water.

HOLLY. No, I've had enough, really, can feel it swishing around in my belly.

CHIMA. Okay.

HOLLY. Least now I can say. That I've eaten...

CHIMA. Nigerian food.

HOLLY....a ball of fire. That shit was unreasonably hot.

CHIMA (*amused*). Must be true what they say – white people can't handle pepper.

HOLLY. Must be. My actual belly button is hurting, is that normal?

CHIMA *is amused.*

Think I'm getting a hernia.

ONOCHIE (*vexed*). Whose fault is that? I told yer what to avoid but yer ignored.

HOLLY. All right.

CHIMA. Ono.

HOLLY. Don't bite me 'ead off.

ONOCHIE *sits there, playing with his bass.*

Excuse his table manners, Linton.

CHIMA. It's okay. Well, I hope this bad experience doesn't put you off Nigerian food for good.

HOLLY. Not a bad one, just a hot one.

Jamaican girl I went to school with. Brought in some chicken jerk one day. I thought that was hot. But compared to what I just had, that chicken jerk was citrusy.

CHIMA *is amused.*

CHIMA. You're funny. Ono, you didn't tell me she was funny. Well, the hot food is something you just can't avoid when you're dealing with black men – (*Smiles.*) no getting around that.

Pause.

HOLLY (*avoiding the awkward moment*). The whole 'eatin' with yer 'ands' thing –

CHIMA. Yeah, I hope that wasn't too strange for you.

HOLLY. Takes getting used to.

CHIMA. Doesn't come natural to you, does it?

HOLLY. Well, I'm used to using cutlery, aren't I.

CHIMA. Of course.

HOLLY. Kinda felt... kinda made me feel a bit... like an animal. (*Laughs.*)

CHIMA. Like an animal – wow.

HOLLY. To be honest, yeah. D'yer know what I mean?

CHIMA. No. No, this is my culture so no.

HOLLY. Don't understand why yer can't just use cutlery is all.

CHIMA. Have you ever... smelt your hand after you've –

HOLLY. Whoa stop. Slow down there, cowboy. Yer not gonna ask summit nasty, are yer?

CHIMA. No! No.

HOLLY. Juss checkin'.

CHIMA. No.

HOLLY. Okay.

Proceed with speed.

CHIMA. Have –

HOLLY. 'Ave I ever smelt me 'and after dot dot dot – hear 'im, Ono.

CHIMA. Have you ever smelt your hand after you've –

HOLLY. D'yer know 'ow odd the beginnin' of that question sounds? Really odd, but go on.

CHIMA. You gonna let me finish / the question or?

HOLLY. Yeah yeah, 'ave a go.

CHIMA. Have you ever smelt your hand, after you've held a scaffolding pole?

HOLLY. Is that a real question?

CHIMA. Think so.

HOLLY. Yes, I 'ave smelt me 'and after 'olding a scaffolding pole. Smells dodgy after I've 'eld a scaffolding pole. Where is this train 'eadin', sorry?

CHIMA. Smells dodgy.

HOLLY. From my experience, yes.

Not that I go 'round grippin' scaffolding poles for a livin' or nothin' – whass yer point, mister?

CHIMA. Using cutlery adds a 'dodgy' taste to food, is my point.

HOLLY. Ah.

Cutlery gives it a funny taste.

CHIMA. Yeah.

HOLLY. Youse ought to try stainless steel then, babe. One-pound shop.

CHIMA. Lick a stainless-steel spoon and try tell me there's no taste.

HOLLY. I beg yer pardon?

CHIMA. Lick. A stainless-steel spoon. And try tell me there's no taste.

Pause.

HOLLY. Might give it a try when I get in but I'm not promisin' nothin'.

CHIMA. There's a good girl.

HOLLY *is shaking her head at* CHIMA.

What?

HOLLY. Don't 'ave many people orderin' me to lick things is all.

CHIMA. Well. You're only young.

ONOCHIE. Uh, '*Linton*', the time is now eleven-twenty so, ya know, familiarise yerself with that door frame as promised.

CHIMA *looks at* ONOCHIE. CHIMA *now stands and is collecting the dishes on the table, placing them in the sink.*

CHIMA (*to* HOLLY). Do you cook?

HOLLY (*laughs*). Must be joking.

ONOCHIE (*getting up*). Come on, Holly.

HOLLY. Couldn't cook to save me life.

CHIMA. So what do you eat every day?

ONOCHIE (*to* HOLLY). Twinkle.

HOLLY *slowly standing.*

HOLLY (*shrugs*). Dunno.

CHIMA. You don't know?

HOLLY. Ono, what do I eat?

ONOCHIE. Fish and chips – let's get on, I'll walk yer back.

HOLLY (*to* CHIMA). Yeah, whatever's around I guess.

CHIMA. So you eat that with cutlery then – knife and fork.

HOLLY. No.

CHIMA. But I thought you said you don't eat with your hands –

HOLLY. Well, it's fish and chips…

CHIMA. Right.

HOLLY. …come on.

CHIMA. You don't feel like an animal when you're eating that, do you? Just the African food.

HOLLY. Not saying that at all.

ONOCHIE. Time to leave now.

CHIMA. Girls that can't cook. Always confuses me.

HOLLY. I live with my old man, yer see. Can't exactly learn off 'im.

CHIMA. Some day you'll need to know how to cook.

HOLLY (*offended*). I will one day but for now I'm just, yer know, sixteen years old. So, pretty much busy enjoying being that really. Which means that sometimes dinner is five or ten Custard Creams.

CHIMA. That's hilarious but let me tell you, if you're with a black man you got to know how to cook, and properly. Fish and chips, beans and mash – that won't run.

HOLLY (*to* ONOCHIE). Is he always this intense?

ONOCHIE. Don't bother with 'im.

CHIMA. Black men like to eat.

HOLLY. Only black men?

ONOCHIE. Linton, that's enough.

CHIMA. Reason why is because we gotta work so damn hard. We're out there trying to make something out of nothing because we start off one pound away from fifty pence.

HOLLY. We're not talking about cooking any more, are we?

ONOCHIE. Holly, leave it.

HOLLY. No, he's starting on me for what? (*To* CHIMA.) I ate yer food, said it were nice even though it nearly killed me, thanked yer, appreciated it –

CHIMA. My animal food, yeah.

HOLLY. For fuck's sake – what is this? Yer calling me a racist?

ONOCHIE. Okay –

HOLLY (*to* CHIMA). Yer not serious, mate.

CHIMA. You're sixteen, you know nothing.

HOLLY. Would I be in this house if I were racist?

ONOCHIE. Both of yers –

CHIMA. Oh, we've had racists in 'ere before, believe me, you wouldn't be the first.

HOLLY (*re:* ONOCHIE). I'm with *'im*, for heaven's sake!

CHIMA. That's the problem!

HOLLY. Yer need help.

CHIMA. And you need a fucking reality check!

ONOCHIE (*to* CHIMA). Oi!

CHIMA. Stupider than I thought, the both you. If you think it'll be easy living after the world's opinion, you're a fucking idiot.

ONOCHIE. Yer don't talk to 'er like that!

CHIMA. You want to understand that this is impossible, you and him.

HOLLY *stands there, she listens to him – what he says rings true to her.*

ONOCHIE. Holly, let's go –

CHIMA. Got your attention now, don't I? You know I'm right. Setting yourselves up for sufferance only. We've lived it under this roof. You should stick with your own kind and – (*To* ONOCHIE.) you should stick with your own kind!

ONOCHIE. That's enough of yer black-power shit –

CHIMA. You both should know better – I mean, you're a nice girl, don't be dumb, this'll ruin your life –

ONOCHIE (*to* CHIMA). Now –

CHIMA. You carry on down this road with this white girl and you're finished –

ONOCHIE. Chim –

CHIMA. You need to end it – end it with each other now, come on.

ONOCHIE. Chim –

CHIMA (*to* ONOCHIE). YOU DON'T WANNA MAKE THE SAME MISTAKE THAT I DID!

ONOCHIE. CHIMA!

CHIMA (*to* HOLLY). YOU DON'T WANNA END UP LIKE MY MUM!

ONOCHIE. CHIMA! Fuck's sake. Just. Calm down.

Pause.

Holly.

ONOCHIE *goes to the door but* HOLLY *doesn't move.*

Let's go.

Beat.

HOLLY *is frozen – staring at* CHIMA –

HOLLY. I knew it.

I bloody well knew it, didn't I? 'E ain' yer cousin.

Beat.

ONOCHIE. No. Yeah 'e is. Course 'e is.

HOLLY. Yer called 'im Chima juss now!

ONOCHIE. No I never.

HOLLY. 'E ain' yer cousin as much as he's yer brother, Ono. I fuckin' knew it.

ONOCHIE. He ain' my brother. I never said Chima. He's Linden.

HOLLY. Yer a liar – yer a fuckin' liar.

ONOCHIE. He ain' my brother, 'e's my cousin, Holly.

HOLLY. Ah God – me and 'im under the same roof – ah God – in the same room, even – feel sick. (*To* CHIMA.) Yer killed my godsister. Fuckin' standing there... don't look at me.

ONOCHIE. This ain't 'im, Holly. This is Linden.

HOLLY (*leaving*). Yer gonna fuckin' pay for this.

ONOCHIE *tries stopping her from leaving – she shrugs him off.*

Get off.

ONOCHIE. I swear it ain' 'im.

HOLLY *leaves – leaving the door open.*

Fuck's sake, Holly.

ONOCHIE *stands there with his hands on his head.*

CHIMA. You didn't think it necessary to tell me from before that she's Old Graham's goddaughter?

ONOCHIE. Yer weren' meant to come downstairs, were yer, yer fuckin'… destroyer. Were yer? Jesus Christ Almighty – yer kill me. Yer kill me dead.

CHIMA. You said my name.

ONOCHIE. It wouldn't 'ave happened – If yer done as yer was asked this wouldn't – oi, where yer going? Oi –

CHIMA *runs out of the door.*

Oi!

ONOCHIE *goes after him.*

Some moments pass.

CHIMA *re-enters, dragging* HOLLY *in – she's trying to scream –* CHIMA *has his hand over her mouth – her legs kicking – trying to get away.*

HOLLY*'s screaming, muffled.*

CHIMA. You're gonna hurt yourself now.

ONOCHIE *slowly following – his hand still on his head – he is gently hysterical.*

ONOCHIE. Ah.

Ah, man.

CHIMA *places her in a chair – still keeps his hand over her mouth.*

Yer gonna do what here, Chim? What's this for?

CHIMA (*to* HOLLY). You gonna calm down.

HOLLY *nods –* CHIMA *takes his hand off her mouth and she takes a deep gasp of air in – she's frightened.*

ONOCHIE. Yer ruined everything.

HOLLY. Don't hurt me. Please…

CHIMA *paces up and down – stressing out.*

CHIMA. I'm not going to hurt you – Ono, shut the door.

ONOCHIE *instinctively, zombie-like, shuts the door.*

ONOCHIE. Yer ruin everything, thass what yer do.

HOLLY. I never done anything to yer.

CHIMA. Shut up, just / sit there quiet, shut up.

ONOCHIE. Make my mum run away, an' now yer juss – yer really pushing the boat out, ain't yer, Chima. Yer want more trouble. Jesus Christ Almighty.

CHIMA. I was trying to protect you.

ONOCHIE. By ruining my life, Chim.

CHIMA. What I'm doing is for your good.

ONOCHIE. Holly, come on, let's go. Holly, up yer get –

CHIMA *goes over and give* ONOCHIE *a powerful slap.*

HOLLY *cowers.*

ONOCHIE *stands there – afraid – holding his face – fragile now.*

CHIMA. Do you want me to die?

Ono, do you want me to die? Answer me.

ONOCHIE *wags his head 'no'.*

Because someone's gonna die tonight if you don't wise up –

HOLLY (*holding back tears*). I don't wanna die.

CHIMA. And I don't want anyone to die. Long as we all do as I say. Then everyone will be fine, I promise. I promise, okay. Cos I just came back to see my brother and my mum, that's all. I didn't want all this. I didn't. So let's all fuckin' do what I say, okay?

HOLLY. Okay.

CHIMA. Nice.

Ono.

Ono, go stand by the door.

ONOCHIE *doesn't move – he still stands there holding his face.*

Go stand by the door, Ono. Stand –

ONOCHIE. Why.

Pause.

CHIMA. STAND IN FRONT OF THE FUCKIN' DOOR!

ONOCHIE. Holly, I don't know what he's doing.

ONOCHIE *stands in front of the door.*

CHIMA (*to* HOLLY). Sit down properly.

HOLLY. I'm not the one yer wanna deal with.

CHIMA. I don't wanna deal with anybody. I'd rather not deal with anyone, I just wanna get the fuck out of here. Get my life back. Cos I don't deserve this.

CHIMA *paces.*

They know I'm here?

HOLLY. They'd already be 'ere if they knew.

CHIMA. Told them I was here?

HOLLY. I've been 'ere with yer lot all evening, 'ow the hellfuck could I 'ave done that?

CHIMA. This why you got involved with my brother?

HOLLY *looks at* ONOCHIE.

Am I the reason you got involved with him, yes or no?

HOLLY. Ain't exactly why but… I was gonna tell 'im today – (*To* ONOCHIE.) This is what I've needed to… Ono, I came to speak to yer 'bout something today.

ONOCHIE. Holly, what the fuck, Holly.

CHIMA. See.

ONOCHIE. Holly!

HOLLY (*rising*). It's what I was saying earlier.

CHIMA. You better sit back down.

ONOCHIE. Yer didn't say anything, Holly!

HOLLY. I said it would be complicated – to be yer girlfriend, Ono, basically Old Graham saw us kissing behind the car park a couple months back and I thought he was gonna do yer some damage but he blackmailed me, Ono – said I was to let 'im know if I 'eard anything 'bout Chima. So I said okay cos I didn't want yer getting hurt, Ono. He said if I didn't do it 'e was gonna 'ave yer cut up, then he'd tell my dad on me an' get me sent to fuckin' Nottingham to live with my mum an' yer know 'ow much I hate that bitch, she'd 'ave never let me come up to see yer – thass all it was, I swear on Poppy's grave. We were already seein' each other, Ono. 'E juss said if I 'eard anythin' I should relay it by 'im – thass all it was. And we 'aven't even spoken about 'im, 'ave we?

(*To* CHIMA.) I 'aven't told 'em yer 'ere. I've 'ad no means to.

Pause.

CHIMA. Ono. Is there any rope in the house?

HOLLY. I'm not even lying.

CHIMA. Ono.

ONOCHIE *can't get words out.*

HOLLY. What yer need rope for?

CHIMA. Ono.

ONOCHIE. There's no rope.

CHIMA. Speak up!

ONOCHIE. The telly cable cos there's no rope.

CHIMA. Go bring me that and then pack your things.

ONOCHIE. Pack my things for what?

Beat.

CHIMA. We're getting the fuck out of Deptford.

Lights to black.

Scene Four

00:15

HOLLY *is tied to the chair – she has recently stopped crying –
still a bit teary and snotty.* ONOCHIE *lights a cigarette on the
stove and puts it in her mouth for her.* (HOLLY *speaks with the
cigarette in her mouth this whole scene.*)

HOLLY. Thank you but…

ONOCHIE *goes to sit back down –*

(*In pain.*) Can't yer loosen the back or summit? Oh my God.
Yer torturing me – (*Cries in pain.*) My aaaaaarm.

I think it's dislocated.

Silence. HOLLY *shakes her head.*

(*Aggressively struggling in the chair.*) I can't fuckin' believe
this!

CHIMA (*offstage, upstairs*). Shut the fuck up!

HOLLY. Nah, yer brother better pack his things quick and let
me go, ya know, cos me dad'll be worried he ain' 'eard from
me an' thass when 'e'll call Old Graham an' they'll come
lookin'. Yer know what he'll do if he finds us like this?

Silence.

I need to go toilet.

I'm serious. It's not sittin' well wimme, that food. I really
need to go, Ono, my – (*Winces in pain.*) ah, my stomach.

ONOCHIE *is doing his best trying not to listen to her – but it's troubling him.*

Ono, please. This ain't fair. Seriously. (*Starts crying again.*) I'm telling yer the truth. Old Graham told me to keep talkin' to yer is all. But I properly like yer, yer know that.

ONOCHIE. I don't know what to believe any more, Holly. Don't think I can trust yer.

HOLLY. Ono? Ono, it's me. Yer love my shyness, remember? I'm the girl yer love and I'm in love with yer back. I've been all made up since I've started bein' with yer, Ono. Ask me girls. They're always askin' why I'm smilin' an' I'm not even allowed to tell them.

ONOCHIE. Stop talking to us, Holly.

HOLLY. God. Ono.

HOLLY *winces in pain – moans.*

I'm gonna soil my knickers, Ono, I really need to go seriously.

Seriously.

Seriously!

Are yer gonna do this to me?! Ono! Ah? I can't believe this. Know what, if yer do this to me, yer juss cold. Yer gonna let me shit meself? Ono, nah, if yer allow this then I were wrong 'bout yer.

I know yer wanna lemme go. Come *with* me, Ono.

ONOCHIE (*weakening*). I ain' allowed to let yer move anywhere, Holly.

HOLLY. Ono! Ono, 'ave yer lost it?!

There's a banging noise from upstairs.

'E's gonna hurt me. Yer know what 'e's capable of. 'E's gonna hurt me like 'e did Poppy. Is that okay with yer? See how he hit yer. Yer protecting 'im over me, yer don't even know 'im –

ONOCHIE. I ain't protecting 'im –

HOLLY. Aaah. My stomach. My stomach.

ONOCHIE. 'Ow do we know yer ain' gonna go straight 'cross to Liam?

HOLLY. Ah my – please yer gotta lemme leave now now now – (*Struggles in chair.*) I'm gonna go on meself. Ono, ple– no no no –

HOLLY *abruptly stops talking and puts her head down – humiliated.*

A foul smell fills the air – ONOCHIE *smells it, he knows what it is.*

ONOCHIE *goes over to* HOLLY. *He unties her.*

ONOCHIE. Sorry –

HOLLY *pushes past him – runs out.* ONOCHIE *by the door –*

(*Watching after her.*) Now, don't go 'cross the road, promise me yer won't go to –

(*Shouting after her.*) Holly, don't go 'cross the road, 'kay?

Holly, where yer – I said don't – where yer – ah, fuckin' 'ell.

Fuck me.

HOLLY! (*Gesturing for her to go away from somewhere.*)

Fuck me.

What yer doing. Shit.

ONOCHIE *paces up and down for some moments – he sits.*

Fuck me.

ONOCHIE *gets up again and looks outside –*

CHIMA *comes in with some luggage in hand – he freezes as he notices* HOLLY *is not in the chair. The sound of the luggage hitting the floor makes* ONOCHIE *jump – he turns around to see* CHIMA *there.*

She said –

CHIMA. Where is she?

ONOCHIE. She said she wasn't gonna go 'cross the road.

CHIMA. Ono, where is she?

ONOCHIE. She's at Liam's. She juss got there.

Yer all right long as yer leave now. Lef' the door open for yer, look –

CHIMA. ONO, WHAT THE FUCK, MAN! I told you to – all you had to do was watch her, that's all you had to do!

ONOCHIE. 'Er stomach, 'er stom–

CHIMA. That was it! The fuck is wrong is with you, ah?

CHIMA *slaps* ONOCHIE *on the head – instinctively* ONOCHIE *pushes* CHIMA.

ONOCHIE. Do not put yer fuckin' 'ands on me again, or I'll –

CHIMA *slaps his head again.*

CHIMA. Or what?

CHIMA *slaps his head again –* ONOCHIE *tries to block it – he pushes* CHIMA.

ONOCHIE. Touch me again an' see what 'appens.

CHIMA *squares up to* ONOCHIE *–* ONOCHIE *suddenly goes to headbutt him – they're fighting – they grapple on the ground –* CHIMA *has the upper hand – he gets* ONOCHIE *in a headlock –* ONOCHIE *tries to wriggle out and the headlock turns into a choke-hold.*

Enter LIAM *– in a white vest, boxers and black boots – he's clearly just got out of bed – he's nervous – out of breath and a bit jumpy – maybe even frightened – watching them fight.* ONOCHIE *and* CHIMA *don't notice him standing there – they're grappling and* LIAM *moves further into the room.*

(*Muffled.*) I can't breathe – I can't brea–

CHIMA *notices* LIAM *there and stands to his feet,* ONOCHIE *stands too – they look at* LIAM *–* ONOCHIE's *nose is bleeding.*

Silence.

LIAM. Sorry, 'ave I stuck me oar into summit?

Didn't mean to.

He stares at CHIMA.

Big Chim, looking good, mate – Phwar.

(*Indicates to* ONOCHIE*'s bleeding nose.*) Yer, uh…

LIAM *backs up towards the door.*

It's 'im!

'E's 'ere, Dad.

(*Leaving to return.*) Hang about, the both a yers…

Got someone out front as well so. Don't do nothin' stupid.

LIAM *leaves again to return.*

Honestly, fellas, juss be calm, all right, don't try nothin' silly, all right, we got yer surrounded – as they say. We don't want it getting messy.

LIAM *runs off.*

Pause.

ONOCHIE. Poison.

Poison.

(*Leaving.*) Thass what you are.

CHIMA. It's just us two, Ono.

ONOCHIE *goes to leave.* CHIMA *tries holding him back but* ONOCHIE *pulls away.*

Me and you.

ONOCHIE. Yer on yer own –

CHIMA. Ono, Mum's not coming back. It's just us.

ONOCHIE *stops.*

She left us this.

CHIMA *takes out of his pocket the note that he tore up and binned earlier – it's taped back together.*

Was in her room. Found it soon as I got in.

Beat.

ONOCHIE. Yer didn't say this to me earlier.

CHIMA. I didn't know how.

ONOCHIE *comes over and takes the note from* CHIMA.

ONOCHIE. Yer tore it up.

CHIMA. –

As ONOCHIE *reads, barking can be heard outside –*

ONOCHIE. She's…

ONOCHIE *wags his head while reading.*

She's apologising to yer for what – yer wrote this, dint yer?

CHIMA. Come on. It's Mum's writing.

ONOCHIE *reads.*

ONOCHIE. Fucking… (*Getting emotional.*) Well, this ain't making any sense, apologising when yer the one who's, uh… (*Reads.*) who's done all this…

CHIMA. It's just us now.

ONOCHIE (*re: note*). Forgive her for what?

CHIMA. You know, man.

ONOCHIE. What yer implying this is saying, Chim? Cos this means nothing. This doesn't mean anything!

CHIMA. She wasn't well, man. Said it yourself, she's been low.

ONOCHIE *starts breaking – knowing* CHIMA *is right.*

ONOCHIE (*breaking down*). Why… why didn't yer show it to me earlier, yer cunt?

CHIMA. Was trying to be strong for you. As she's called us to be in that letter, strong for each other. We have to do right by her.

ONOCHIE (*breaking down*). Yer... *agreed* with me earlier, yer agreed, that that... if I didn't 'ear from 'er by tomorrow...

CHIMA. Sorry.

ONOCHIE (*crying*). Yer said I shouldn't think like that. But yer... (*Points to the note.*) all along... fucking... see? The deceit in yer eyes – I knew yer were hiding something...

CHIMA. I'm sorry.

ONOCHIE (*crying*). Bit late for that, man.

ONOCHIE *puts his head on the table – he is weeping like this.*

LIAM *returns – walks further into the kitchen – he draws the curtain aside – looks out back.*

LIAM. Yer ought see this – (*Holds the curtain aside.*)

Pure bully out there, look. Pure muscle. Holding pavement. An' what is it, one what... (*Checks wristwatch.*) One forty a.m. (*Looks outside, counts.*) One two three four five six seven eight nine ten eleven twelve...

Twelve of Deptford's most armsy hottin' up yer back door. It's really eleven an' a half though innit cos Lil' Ronan's out there. 'E's only a little bit. Short as 'is temper though. Yer can't tell 'im 'is fuckin' short, 'e'll fuckin'... stab yer in the calf.

Don't know why yer didn't juss stay away, Chima. Wha'd yer think would 'appen?

Dad's calling yer out.

I remember the first time I were called out. I didn't wanna go. Yer remember this story. Were only eight years old. Get called out by me own cousin. 'E's eleven at the time, 'ad three years on me. Now I'd been stealing from 'im 'is pocket money. Right from under 'is nose for weeks. 'Is savings. Ya see he had this framed Beatles poster up on his wall. Bored one day, I accidentally dash a tennis ball at it. The picture of the Fab Four comes down an' with it, some pound coins I discovered. His hiding place. He was lining up pound coins

on the inside of the picture frame. Well, when I were eatin'
more Haribo an' chocolate mice than the pocket money me
mum gave me could afford an' it came to surface that I were
a thievin' little shit. 'E calls me out. I cry me little eyes out
cos e's a lot bigger than me. Me dad says, 'Yer gotta face the
consequences to yer actions, young man,' as 'e drags me out
into the street – just out there – the whole community waitin'
– like they are right now. I'm crying buckets. Me cousin in
the middle, waiting with 'is dukes up. An' soon as me dad le'
go of me wrist I make a break for it. But, Chima – (*Laughs.*)
hear this, I'm so terrified, Chima, that I run right into a
postbox. Straight into a postbox! When I come back around,
me cousin gives me a few slaps, not so bad as the postbox.
Come out an' get yer slaps, mate. Or else yer'll have the
postbox.

Graham's asked that yer come outside, Chim – it's the law of
the land. We were talking juss now an' 'e's asked me to escort
yer outside. I ask 'im, 'Dad, why'd yer need *me* to do this?'
Well, 'e's notion from thinking is that 'e didn't wanna send
any old muscle to do it. Dad's got class now, know what I
mean? He wants only to send someone who knows yer
personally, a familiar face, 'Thass why I send you,' 'e says.
So I tells 'im, I'll fetch yer. But only on my stipulations.
'Dad. Me an' Chima go way back. He was my best friend.
The best friend I ever 'ad. Anyone else, any old fucker, an' I'll
drag 'im outta bed along with 'is missus, I'll drag 'im out 'is
mother's womb, outta eleven o'clock mass, exhume 'im from
'is grave or what 'ave yer, it's nothin'. But I can't with Chim.
Because Chim *knows* the protocol. Besides, it juss wouldn't
feel right. I ain't *grabbin'* Chima,' I tells 'im. 'Chima knows
what 'appens if 'e doesn't come outside. 'E is familiar the
repercussions. I'll *ask* 'im. Nicely,' I says 'I'll ask 'im, nicely,
an' if Chim, doesn't wanna walk 'imself out, well then, 'e is
fully aware 'e 'as contravened a long-established, time-
honoured, decree of Eddon Road. Of which, the punishments
are draconian.' 'E's called yer out, mate. Yer gotta go. Yer
gotta face the consequences to yer actions.

Yer caused a death. It wouldn't be so wrong as to say that yer
murdered my little sister, Chim. We all thought we knew yer

– me the most. Sixteen years old she was. Gone. Gone. Not an explanation from yer. Not an apology. We fuckin' – didn't we always treat yer like yer was one of us, Chim? Sylvia raised yer like yer were one of her own.

Yer broke many hearts. People made up their minds that night. They said if yer stepped again yer foot on this turf, yer a dead man. Why would yer come back 'ere for?

LIAM *looks through the curtain.*

More of 'em gatherin'.

Dad's orders: if yer don't come out, 'e'll board yer house up, with yer in it, an' 'e'll burn it down, with yer in it. That was the deal. I stood up for yer already, mate – as much as I could. When 'e said we ought drag yer out I said, 'No, this is Chim.' So I thinks yer ought to come outsides wimme, Chim, mate.

LIAM *holds open the door.*

I'm not in the business of begging! Yer gonna be a man or a coward? Stay in 'ere an' it is Barbecue Boulevard.

Beat.

Right.

I've said me wordage.

LIAM *starts going through all of the cupboards – he finds what he's looking for – the liquor and the wine. He lays the bottles out across the table.*

Of all the time I told yer that yer drank too much – yer never could handle yer drink, not like yer dad – this is the one time that I'd encourage yer get bladdered. Cock back a mighty swig of all them. If it's any consolation to yer, I ain' joinin' in. Numb yourself a bit. An' come meet us outside.

LIAM *goes to leave –*

CHIMA. I saw Sylvia yesterday. In the morning. At the graveyard.

LIAM *stops.*

She had two bunches of flowers. I was watching her from far off. She was there first, I felt to give her her time with Poppy, you know… I know she saw me. Well off in the distance I was standing but I know she knew it was me. She waved my way as she was leaving.

LIAM. Is that right.

CHIMA. Too far away to see my face but she knew it was me – do you know how?

LIAM. Give it a rest, yer ain't talking yer way out of this.

CHIMA. She knew because in these hands, I was holding two bunches of flowers also. Just like her.

LIAM. –

CHIMA. It has to be two. A big bunch – smaller one.

You've buried my blood.

I didn't kill them.

Beat.

LIAM. What yer sayin'?

CHIMA. I didn't kill them.

LIAM. You're sayin' them.

CHIMA. You've buried my blood.

LIAM. –

CHIMA. Poppy was my girl and she was having our child.

LIAM. Yer sick.

CHIMA. We told my mum first, me and Poppy –

LIAM. Yer sick.

CHIMA. Then Sylvia came over –

LIAM. Yer an' Poppy.

CHIMA. Couldn't tell you about it, best mates or not. Couldn't have it getting to your dad. And hiding happiness from the people you love… that's tougher than hiding sadness, believe, but we did it. For over a year. We lied. You know, Liam, when Poppy started to show I was kind of glad at first. I thought it meant we wouldn't need to lie any more. Turned out meaning the complete opposite.

LIAM. Is this what yer sayin' now, yer fuckin' sicko.

CHIMA. Yer mum knows the truth.

LIAM. Fuck off.

CHIMA. It's why she's been an angel to us after.

LIAM. Right, thass it – no more outta yer!

CHIMA. She visited me – Sylvia was the only one who visited.

LIAM. Another word outta yer and thass it!

CHIMA. Know what she came and said to me? Know what she said? Nothing. She couldn't get a word out for all her sobbing. Cos she knows it weren't my crime. The only crime I done was love Poppy.

LIAM. I was there in court, yer sad prick, yer forgotten?

CHIMA. Your dad, wanders in here after Poppy and Sylvia, two in the morning it was. Four of us around that table. Sylvia bursts into tears before we even start telling him. Imploring your old man to have mercy.

LIAM. Yer lying –

CHIMA. He looses his nut. Reaches over and tries to strangle me. Sylvia begging him. My mum pleading. They cling on to his arms but he shakes them off – marches across back to yours. Comes back with a baseball bat.

LIAM. Thass enough.

CHIMA. He swings for me with everything he had Old Graham, and our Poppy.

LIAM. CHIM!

CHIMA. Our Poppy got in the way. Because she didn't like the violence.

LIAM. –

CHIMA. Your old man cracked her skull wide open with that
one swing. She was done. She didn't make any sound. She
just fell. That was it. So don't tell me who I killed –

CHIMA *is stepping towards* LIAM –

Cos my mum and your mum shed a fucking river! Of tears,
as they together, on their knees, washed Poppy's blood away
from the tile you're standing on – right there. Old Graham
got his way again. He wanted to see blood and he got it. But
you'd have thought the blood was his the way he was
carrying on. Never seen a man like that before, let alone, a
man like your dad, who was always standing upright in my
sights – lying on his back, squirming around, crying like a
child and pulling out his hair. Now, Poppy died saving me
because that swing was intended for *my* noggin. So when
your dad picks himself up, he reckons that I'm half to blame
for this. And I don't think I am. That is until my own mother
begs me to take the bullet. My mum. I reckon her way of
thinking at the time was that the best thing – cos I was
fucked regardless, although I did nothing I was fucked, a
white girl is dead under a black man's roof and when it's his
word against mine it's an open-and-shut case – Mum thought
it was best to salvage what she had left. That sorry case right
there – (*Re:* ONOCHIE.) reckon she had her concentrates on
that boy, his future, so he don't have to suffer. In the moment
I agree to take the bullet – listen, I was only eighteen years
old, my girlfriend laying dead in front of me, her forehead
yawning, my beautiful girl, in an ever-growing pool of claret,
your dad promising this and that – I agreed in a moment
where I was unfit to think for myself. Not an informed
decision, do you understand? I agreed to take the rap but
fuck me, I didn't agree to this. I didn't agree to the
arrangement of my being stabbed to death in prison. And I
didn't agree to you and your lot turning my fucking gem of a
brother, who used to adore me, into a little racist prick who
hates the colour of his own fucking skin. No, your dad
promised to take care of my mum but truth has it he ain't so
much as acknowledged her, if you don't include him spitting
her way in court, that is – MY MOTHER'S GONE NOW!

My mother's gone, it's taken both my parents, this hatred. My family, ripped apart. And your old man, disloyal racist cunt murderer.

CHIMA *gets very close to* LIAM, *who is afraid of him.*

LIAM. Keep back.

CHIMA. And you've known.

LIAM *starts to break down.*

You knew and all. You've known this. Haven't you. All this time. Just say that you did. Just admit that you did.

LIAM, *full of emotion, slumps down to the floor.*

Yeah, sit down cos you knew, man. Your whole family know the truth. Could've spoke up for me but you never did. Turned your back on me. Some best mate you are.

LIAM (*emotional – covering his face*). I'm sorry. I'm sorry.

CHIMA *picks him up.*

CHIMA. You 'fraid him more than any of us ever did, cos he kicked the shit outta you with regularity, but you'll talk to him for us. Okay? Talk to him. Tell him we've had enough. He can't take any more off us. Tell him to leave us alone.

LIAM. Yer know 'im, Chim –

CHIMA. Listen!

LIAM. He ain' gonna budge, Chim.

CHIMA. He won't if you don't ask him. Liam? Liam! It's your fucking one chance to not be lackey.

LIAM. –

CHIMA. Ey?

LIAM. Yer know 'im. 'E won't call it off.

CHIMA. The way I feel I could kill you right where you stand just for worshipping the cunt – you can fuck off! (*Pushing him out.*) Youse better be ready for a battle – and I'm killing those dogs and all.

CHIMA *throws* LIAM *out.* CHIMA *walks over to the drink on the table. He opens a bottle.*

Ono.

ONOCHIE *still sits at the table in a daze.*

CHIMA *puts the bottle to his lips and drinks it till it's half-empty.*

You're gonna have to leave out of here.

CHIMA *leaves the room – he returns.*

Out front as well. Whole army of them. The pillars of our great community.

CHIMA *takes another swig and the bottle is empty. Coughs.*

You need to get out of here, man.

CHIMA *opens up another bottle – starts on that one.*

Leave and just keep walking. You don't wanna see what'll happen to them. I'm gonna dead them all.

CHIMA *looks through the curtain.*

Twenty dead snowflakes.

CHIMA *finishes that bottle.*

I know you got a spliff on you, right.

CHIMA *goes into* ONOCHIE*'s shirt pocket –* ONOCHIE *is still motionless, in a daze.*

Part of being a skin.

CHIMA *pulls a short roach-spliff out of* ONOCHIE*'s pocket –*

(*Sotto.*) Nothing to do with your fucking wisdom tooth.

He lights it on the stove – smokes it – drinks some more.

If you're wise you'll get on, little brother, get up.

CHIMA *paces up and down.*

CHIMA *takes another swig from a bottle – winces in distaste.*

Wooo! Get it in.

Can't afford to memorise the send-off I'm about to give these cunts. You understand? Blood of twenty men on my mind – (*Smokes.*) how I'm gonna sleep tomorrow – (*Shrugs.*)

Not taking this one sitting down. No fucking chance.

CHIMA *looks at his brother and, breaking down –*

Beautiful. Hear what I'm telling you, little brother, you're beautiful. You're beautiful, everything about you is. Believe that. And one day they're gonna be so ashamed! So ashamed of themselves for thinking any different – (*Wipes his eyes, trying to stop himself from crying.*) ah...

Sorry I haven't been here for you, man.

ONOCHIE *suddenly quickly stands and slams into his brother, hugging him tight –* CHIMA *is taken aback. They hug.*

ONOCHIE. I'm sorry.

CHIMA. Nah.

They continue hugging.

You better go.

CHIMA *pats* ONOCHIE*'s back until they stop hugging.*

CHIMA *takes to another bottle.* ONOCHIE *still stands there.*

Ah, Mum. I've spent forever... hating Mum. She's taken the easy way out again.

ONOCHIE. Mum didn't say all those things about yer, that yer weren't her son and that. That's the way *I've* felt. She'd try talking about yer sometimes, I didn't wanna hear about it, man. It was me.

CHIMA....She could've come once. At least once.

ONOCHIE. Reckon she'd 'ave been ashamed in 'erself. She said she's sorry for it.

CHIMA (*takes another swig*). Done now anyway.

ONOCHIE. Yeah, cos… that regret you were saying about. She'd be full of it.

Pause.

CHIMA. You're too intelligent for Eddon Street.

This is why I gotta kill 'em all.

ONOCHIE. Save one for me, ey.

CHIMA *is trying not to cry.*

CHIMA. Ahhh! Fuck!

You've gotta go, man.

CHIMA *tries to push* ONOCHIE *out of the door.*

ONOCHIE. No, hold on –

CHIMA. They won't touch you.

ONOCHIE. I wanna help yer.

CHIMA (*pushing him out*). I don't need help, / go go go.

ONOCHIE. I'm stayin' 'ere. Move, get off me. I'm stayin'.

CHIMA. You can't help, Ono!

ONOCHIE *is not budging* – CHIMA *sits somewhere – he is not crying.*

ONOCHIE. Ten year. Yer the stupidest person I know. Why yer didn't juss say to me soon as yer got 'ere.

CHIMA. I wrote you a thousand times.

ONOCHIE. And a thousand time yer failed to mention yer never done it, Chim. Thass a big thing to leave out.

CHIMA. You read them.

ONOCHIE. I ain' illiterate. Yer made 'em out to me, dint yer.

CHIMA. Ono, I didn't do it.

ONOCHIE. A little late in the day, Chim, don't you think? Should've said this to the judge ten year ago, pal. Cashing that cheque in… yer don't spend a decade serving another man's time, yer mug. And leaving me… but I'm sorry… I know, all right? I know.

CHIMA *drinks more and more.*

Mum's juss as thick and all, asking yer to do it.

CHIMA *relights the spliff on the stove.*

CHIMA. Ptshh…

These white boys are about to catch the beat-down of their lives! Gonna go outside and lynch them with their own rope. All down Eddon Street. Two man per tree.

CHIMA *suddenly can no longer take it – he flips out, moving around the space for something to break –*

AHHHHHHHH!

CHIMA *pulls himself into a ball – his fingers pulling at his afro – he hyperventilates.*

ONOCHIE *wanders over to his brother – not knowing what to do – he's emotional – something comes over him.*

ONOCHIE. Fuck it.

ONOCHIE *goes over to the table – grabs a bottle and starts drinking it quickly – it stings his chest. He coughs and* CHIMA *looks to him.*

CHIMA. What you doing?

ONOCHIE. We're gonna ride this one out together.

CHIMA. Nah, Ono –

ONOCHIE. No, lissen. I'm a stand-up guy –

CHIMA *is being very forceful and rough with* ONOCHIE, *dragging him to the door.*

CHIMA. MOVE!

ONOCHIE. Ain' letting yer go out there on yer own.

Brother.

ONOCHIE *has managed to wriggle away – he picks up a bottle.*

I'll take 'alf the beatin' on my back and yer'll take the other.

ONOCHIE *takes a swig – winces – jumps on the spot, warming up.*

We'll lynch 'em together.

ONOCHIE *gets down – does ten push-ups –*

ONOCHIE *bounces to his feet – holds his hand out for* CHIMA *to pass him the spliff –*

Pass de kutchie on de lef'-hand side.

Something has faded up in time for...

Scene Five

01:05...

This scene comes immediately after Scene Four, almost conjoined to the end of it.

Loud reggae music pumps –

The scene is stylistic/dream-like, with dance and movement between the brothers.

They're drinking.

They're smoking.

Progressively getting higher and drunker.

The bass is thumping.

ONOCHIE *ceremoniously removes his Ben Sherman shirt and bins it.*

Removes his suspenders and bins them.

Removes his Dr. Martens and bins them.

CHIMA*'s shirt is open – prison scars on show.*

CHIMA *beckons* ONOCHIE *over. They shout over the music.*

CHIMA. What's… what's your favourite thing in the world?

ONOCHIE. Being with my brother.

CHIMA. Aw, man. Aw, man.

> CHIMA *wants to cry.*

You mean that?

ONOCHIE. Yeah.

CHIMA. You're not just saying that because I'm here.

ONOCHIE (*dancing off*). Nah.

CHIMA. Come here. We have something in common then, because you're my favourite thing too.

ONOCHIE. Yeah?

> CHIMA *pulls their foreheads together.*

CHIMA. God knows it's true.

ONOCHIE. I love yer.

CHIMA. Ah, man – (*Holding back tears.*)

> I love you so much, bro.

> I love you, man.

ONOCHIE. Yeah.

> *With the reggae music blaring and the brothers at centre stage.*

> *Lights slowly ease into blackness…*

> *The End.*

A Nick Hern Book

God's Property first published in Great Britain in 2013 as a paperback original by Nick Hern Books Limited, The Glasshouse, 49a Goldhawk Road, London W12 8QP, in association with Talawa Theatre Company, Soho Theatre, London, and the Albany, Deptford

God's Property copyright © 2013 Arinze Kene

Arinze Kene has asserted his right to be identified as the author of this work

Cover photograph by Helen Maybanks
Cover image design by Michael Windsor-Ungureanu
Cover design by Ned Hoste, 2H

Typeset by Nick Hern Books, London
Printed in Great Britain by Mimeo Ltd, St Ives, Cambs PE27 3LE

A CIP catalogue record for this book is available from the British Library

ISBN 978 1 84842 325 1

www.nickhernbooks.co.uk

facebook.com/nickhernbooks

twitter.com/nickhernbooks